The Whale Book

Whales and other marine animals
as described by Adriaen Coenen in 1585

edited with an introduction
by Florike Egmond and Peter Mason
with commentaries by Kees Lankester

REAKTION BOOKS

Published by Reaktion Books Ltd
79 Farringdon Road
London EC1M 3JU, UK

www.reaktionbooks.co.uk

First published 2003

Introduction and edited text copyright © Florike Egmond and Peter Mason, 2003
Commentaries copyright © Kees Lankester, 2003

Photographs by Dries van den Brande, © 2003 of the Royal Zoological Society of Antwerp

The generous sponsorship of the Dutch Ministry of Agriculture, Nature Management and Fisheries, the World Wide Fund for Nature, Greenpeace and the International Fund for Animal Welfare is acknowledged.

Designed by Ron Costley
Typeset by Jill Burrows
Printed in Hong Kong

British Library Cataloguing in Publication Data

Coenen, Adriaen
  The whale book : whales and other marine animals as
  described by Adriaen Coenen in 1585
  1. Whales – Early works to 1800 2. Marine animals – Early
  works to 1800 3. Manuscripts, Dutch 4. Illumination of books
  and manuscripts, Dutch
  I. Title II. Egmond, Florike III. Mason, Peter, 1952–
  IV. Lankester, Kees
  599.5

ISBN 1 86189 174 1

Self-portrait of Adriaen Coenen as a sea knight (from his *Fish Book*). The name Schilperoort on the banner indicates his descent on his mother's side. The three shells are his family device.

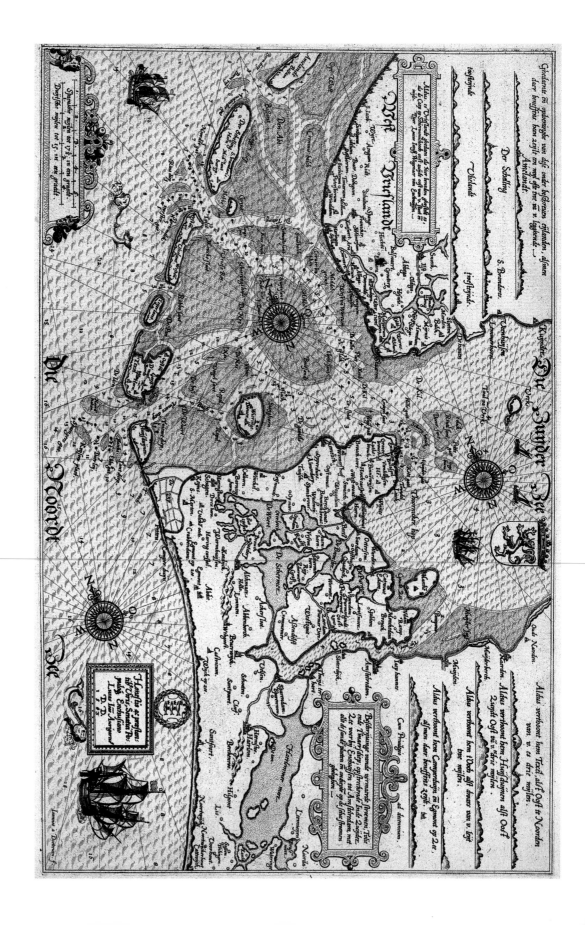

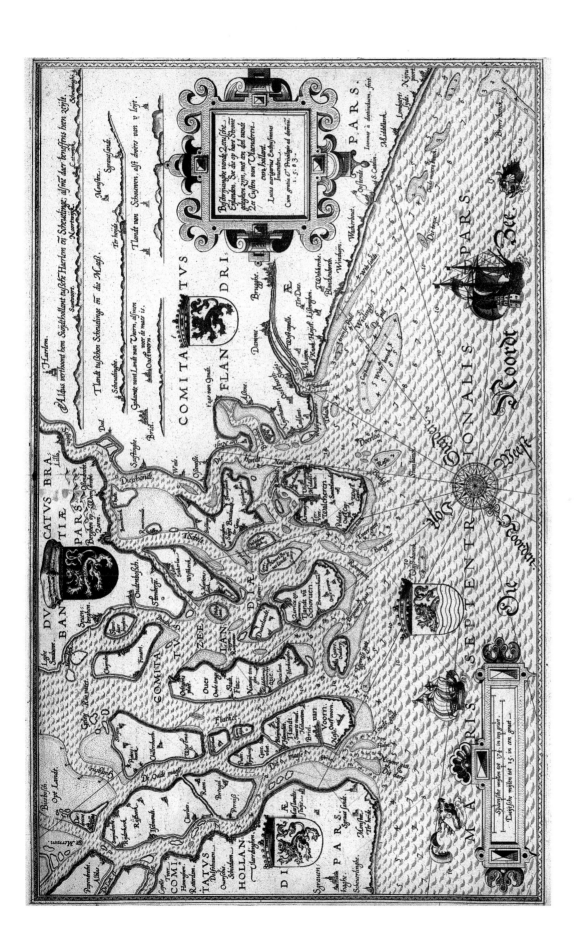

The provinces of Holland and Zeeland, from Lucas Wagenaer van Enkhuizen,
Spieghel der Zeevaerdt, Enkhuizen, 1584.
Note that the orientation of the map, as in Coenen's renderings of the Dutch coastline,
has been rotated by about 110° in an anti-clockwise direction.

Introduction

Adriaen Coenen, the son of a Dutch fisherman, lived almost half a millennium ago, from 1514 to 1587. This is his first publication. *The Whale Book*, which he began in 1584 and completed two years before his death, is probably one of the oldest manuscripts in the world to be entirely devoted to whales and other marine mammals, fish and other creatures that lived in the waters of northwest Europe. *The Whale Book* is one of the three extant illustrated manuscripts by Coenen. These albums, with their numerous, brightly coloured watercolour illustrations, have always been unique. Immediately after their production they were appreciated and regarded as rare and unusual, but in the course of their subsequent history they have never been accessible to more than a few. This is the first publication to present an international public with a selection from the creatures of the sea as they were seen, described and above all represented by a self-made man with a lifetime's experience of fish and fishing.

Adriaen Coenen was no scholar, but he was an expert who managed to combine his practical experience as a fisherman's son, clerk of the fish auction and wholesaler in fish with the information that was available in the main international scholarly publications on fish and marine mammals of his day. He did not own these publications, but had access to them via a rich fellow villager. That combination of everyday practical experience and specialized knowledge is not the only thing that makes Coenen's albums so special. Although Coenen's only son, Coenraet van Schilperoort (1577–1635/6), was to become a

landscape painter (he was connected with the same artistic circles in Leiden as Rembrandt and Jan van Goyen), his father was certainly no great artist. All the same, his watercolours (which are in many cases accurate enough to enable present-day naturalists to identify the species in question) are fascinating for their use of colour and style, and the unmistakable flair with which he set to work. Typical of the three extant illustrated manuscripts is the combination of framed textual passages, rich illustrations with a striking use of colour (Coenen used ochre, green, red, pink, purple, brown and black water-based paints), and above all the naïve and extremely lively idiom of both the illustrations and the texts. On occasion Coenen even composed delightful little poems. Almost every page is an individual, self-contained unit, bound by its decorated margins, and contains one or more watercolour drawings. Coenen's albums radiate the pleasure he must have felt in compiling them, and five centuries on they still possess a charm to which no reader or viewer will be immune.

Besides that charm, Coenen's manuscripts are also important for their place within the history of the natural sciences. Coenen was not the only person to compile manuscripts of this kind in the sixteenth century. Marcus zum Lamm (1544–1606), for example, compiled three manuscript volumes with texts and watercolour illustrations of birds (largely based on the work of Conrad Gessner), and Anselmus de Boodt (1550–1632) likewise produced three albums of nature drawings. But Marcus zum Lamm was a Protestant cleric at the court of the Prince Electors of the Palatinate in Heidelberg, and Anselmus de

Boodt was court physician to Emperor Rudolf II in Prague. What is so unique about Coenen's manuscripts is that they did not arise in a courtly setting. On the contrary, they are pre-eminently important for offering us a glimpse into a creative workshop where 'popular' knowledge fused with the learned tradition of natural historical writing to produce something new.

Moreover, much of the specific information that Coenen's manuscripts provide is without parallel. His account and illustrations of the exotic sunfish, for instance, may be the very first of their kind in Europe. As the famous art historian Ernst Gombrich once demonstrated, the ways in which printers of illustrated works transposed engravings from one context to another in the sixteenth century meant that the resulting images tended to be generic rather than specific. This is equally true of many of the engravings of beached whales that circulated in Coenen's day: there are several instances of the recycling of a ready-to-hand image of a beached whale to illustrate a stranding in another place and time. Seen against this background, the specificity and degree of detail of Coenen's texts and illustrations showing which fish, sea mammals and other marine creatures lived in the North Sea and the adjacent Atlantic Ocean in the sixteenth century are remarkable. He thus offers rare insights into that time-span of climatic change around 1580 that introduced the culmination of the Little Ice Age in Europe. The watercolours in *The Whale Book*, for example, show how many different kinds of whales he was acquainted with, and the texts make it clear how much he knew about them. He mentions and illustrates the schools of whales that passed through the North Sea almost every year; they could be seen at various points along the Dutch coast, and sometimes stranded and perished on its beaches. Indeed, the phenomenon of beached whales was a frequent occurrence on these shores during the second half of the sixteenth century. The work also contains fascinating details about the techniques and technologies of sixteenth-century fishing for plaice, herring, flounder and cod, as well as about fishing for types that are extinct in the North Sea today, such as sturgeon and salmon. His comments on the relation between the movements of shoals of fish and changes in the meteorological conditions or the flight of certain birds make him an early forerunner of ecological studies.

At the same time, Coenen's world was in many ways radically different from our world today. Perhaps this emerges most clearly in the fact that he includes creatures that are nowadays regarded as belonging to myth and fable, but whose existence, though called into doubt in the sixteenth century, had not been definitively disproved. Coenen represents them, while at the same time displaying his own critical acumen by the common addition of the rider: 'I know this from hearsay, but I have never myself seen it.' Rational scepticism was not confined to the circles of the learned in Renaissance Europe.

Although Coenen and his contemporaries were well aware of the distinction between cold-blooded fish and warm-blooded viviparous mammals, the use of the term 'fish' to cover both categories may seem confusing.

However, a brief glance at the range of subject-matter covered in the manuscripts is enough to show that Coenen had little interest in the systems of classification that were such a preoccupation of many of his more learned contemporaries. Nor was he the kind of person to restrict his focus to marine matters alone. The illustration of a particular fish often prompts him to digress on all kinds of subjects that a modern reader would hardly expect to find within the pages of a book about the sea and its fauna: the details of how to prepare a sole, fishing techniques, legends associated with sirens and mermaids, the migratory patterns of schools of herrings in the North Sea, the crocodiles in the Nile, how dolphins give birth to and nourish their young, creatures of the Far East and the Americas, sea monsters, bats and aquatic spirits, all tumble over one another in the pages of his manuscripts.

It is precisely these anecdotes, however, that make Coenen's albums so valuable as a source for the broader cultural history of the sixteenth century. These accompanying texts are full of intriguing, fascinating, lively, original and sometimes amusing observations that offer insights into both the everyday and the dramatic events of life in the Northern Netherlands. Thus we read the shocked reaction of an Italian nobleman to the news that the Dutch ate raw fish: 'O what kind of people would they be to go to war with? One would not dare to cook them any food.' The public execution at the stake of two murderers comes in for an *en passant* comment because Coenen remarks that the men used to fish near Scheveningen. And there is the story of

the man from Egmond who was hanged in England for selling an inedible shark as a sturgeon. Time and again, the personal intertwines with the grander political stage: when a young whale is stranded near Scheveningen in 1581, the event becomes the scene of a meeting between Coenen (armed with his *Fish Book*) and William of Orange, the leader of the Dutch revolt against Spain. On this occasion, the Dutch leader spoke to Coenen's son (who was about four years old at the time) and gave him a gold coin – an indication of the ease with which Coenen managed to move among different social classes. Coenen's visit to an inn in The Hague where captive Inuit from the Labrador coast were on display prompts him to mention the iconoclastic fury of 1566. A plea for unity among Christians and the end of the religious disputes is understandable from a man who had experienced the Reformation at close quarters, grown up in a Habsburg state with the burning of heretics and the persecution of Anabaptists, and ended his life in the new Republic of the North Netherlands, which had an official policy of religious tolerance. But it is characteristic of Coenen that his plea is embedded in a series of brief remarks on the Revelation of St John and the seven-headed monster that emerged from the sea – a marine monster that was a 'must' for his albums.

THE MAN AND HIS WORK

Who was this intriguing Adriaen Coenen? And how did he come to produce such extraordinary albums? His full name was Adriaen Coenensz. van Schilperoort, and he was born in Scheveningen on the Dutch coast near The Hague in 1514 to a fisherman from the same village and a fisherman's daughter from a neighbouring coastal village. The countless references in his writings to 'our village of Scheveningen,' 'our Holland' and 'our land of Holland, Zeeland and Flanders' are a clear enough indication that he felt close bonds with his native village and with the province of Holland. He served as an apprentice to the auctioneer of the Scheveningen fish market and slowly worked his way up to become clerk of the auction – a public function that demanded literacy, a knowledge of financial affairs, and a certain level of prosperity in connection with the advance payments made to fishers – wholesaler in dried and fresh fish, official 'beachcomber' of a stretch of the Dutch coast in the province of South Holland, and village dignitary. In 1580 he tried (without success) to turn the post of village dignitary into a family sinecure by having his son appointed as his successor, but after extensive investigations and hearings, the Estates of Holland decided that the function would rotate after Coenen's death as it had done before his appointment.

Apart from a few business trips to neighbouring Brabant and to the Rhineland, Coenen spent all his life in or near Scheveningen. This limited geographical radius did not prevent him from being touched by the dramatic religious, political and military events of his day. After all, the sixteenth century was one of the most turbulent periods in European history. Coenen was born shortly before the division that split Christendom after Martin Luther's protest against the practice of indulgences in the Roman Catholic Church in 1517. A native of the northern province of Holland, he grew up in a world in which both the Northern and the Southern Netherlands formed part of the great Habsburg Empire under Charles V. During his life he witnessed the Reformation, culminating in the iconoclastic fury that swept through the Low Countries in 1566, as well as the related outbreak of the first of a series of Dutch revolts against Habsburg Spain. These would eventually lead to a division between the Protestant North Netherlands centred on Amsterdam and the Spanish South Netherlands centred on Antwerp. Coenen was not an active opponent to Habsburg rule, but neither did he entertain sympathies with Spain. He assumed a middle-of-the-road position in religious disputes too. He was certainly not in favour of the persecution of heretics, and once the Dutch revolt was under way he became a supporter of the Republic and of William of Orange.

The turbulence of the times affected his financial situation as well as his personal safety, career and collection. Coenen refers on at least one occasion to the threat of bankruptcy. During the summer of 1573 he had to flee from freebooting Spanish soldiers and leave his home in Scheveningen, fully expecting to find only ransacked ruins upon his return. Nor were his fears unfounded: his wartime losses included a smoked and salted barnacle-goose as well as a shark, which had been dried and stuffed by Coenen himself, together with the 24 young sharks found in its belly; it had been left hanging in his garden when plundering Spanish soldiers approached. He was not a man to shirk the responsibilities that his position brought him, and when Scheveningen was hit by floods that destroyed part of the village in 1570, Coenen took personal action to provide relief and to restore the damage that had been done. In return, of course, his position and the activities related to it brought him prestige, and he was undoubtedly proud of the fact that he had risen from the rank of a humble son of a fisherman to that of a local administrator and marine expert who was consulted by gentlemen and scholars. By now he was being invited to dine at the tables of the elite; although hardly an equal, he was received as a distinguished and much appreciated guest. He died in 1587, when his only son was just ten years old. We do not know where he was buried.

Adriaen Coenen wrote three book-length works, two of which are still extant. We do not know exactly when he started writing, but it may be deduced from comments in his second manuscript that his first *Fish Book* was already sufficiently elaborated to be presented to interested readers in the 1560s. In 1574 he gave this *Fish Book* as a present to William of Orange, leader of the Dutch Revolt against Spanish Habsburg rule. The fate of this manuscript is still a mystery. His second manuscript, which he later referred to as his *Big Fish Book*, contains 412 folios and was written between 1577 and early 1579. The bound manuscript has been in the possession of the Royal Library in The Hague since the late eighteenth or early nineteenth century. It is currently being restored and digitized. His third work is *The Whale Book* now in the library of the Royal Zoological Society in Antwerp, from which the present publication has been compiled. It consists of two volumes, but it is clear from the concluding page of the second volume that Coenen intended to continue it with at least one more volume. It is not certain whether the slender, unfinished manuscript known as the *Herring King Book*, now in the Cologne Municipal Archive, should be regarded as a third part of *The Whale Book*, or whether it is a separate work. The Cologne manuscript consists mainly of excerpts from Coenen's other manuscripts.

Since none of Coenen's manuscripts has ever been published before – in his own lifetime they were known only to a limited number of people – it can hardly be said that they exerted an impact on the study of nature of his day or had any subsequent influence. Nor can he be regarded as someone who transferred the ideas and conceptions of one generation to the next, or from scholars to common people. The manuscripts have little to offer on this point. What they do show, however, are the forms of knowledge that were accessible to a man who did not belong to the elite of sixteenth-century Holland, and especially *how* he read and integrated knowledge drawn from his reading and his practical experience into a more or less orderly whole in a manner that is both highly personal and also typical of the sixteenth century.

Like most Dutch children, Coenen attended the village school, but that was all the formal education he received. He certainly picked up a considerable number of Latin names for fauna over the years (many of which can still be found in the Linnaean classification system introduced almost two centuries later), although he repeatedly emphasized in his writings that he could not read Latin. He himself wrote in a racy and by no means academic Dutch, seasoned with quotations in Latin, French and German. Besides the Bible and *The Book of Sidrac* (an imaginary dialogue between the court philosopher Sidrac and the King of Bactria on details of biblical lore that was first translated into Dutch in the fourteenth century), he quotes from Pliny, Aelian, Augustine, Isidore, Albertus Magnus and *The Travels* of Sir John Mandeville. However, his access to such classical or medieval authors was through later compilations in the vernacular, such as *Der dieren palleys* (Palace of Animals), the Dutch-language version of a popular compilation of animal lore, Johannes Heyden's German version of Books 7 to 11 of Pliny the Elder's *Historia naturalis*, or Cornelius Aurelius' immensely popular translation and adaptation into Dutch of a Latin chronicle of the States of Holland and Utrecht. He followed the same procedure for many sixteenth-century sources on natural history, such as Guillaume Rondelet, Pierre Belon, Olaus Magnus, Sebastian Münster and Conrad Gessner (the last in a German translation by Cunrat Forer), drawing both on their textual information and on the woodcut engravings that their works contained. Besides works of natural history, his reading and copying also extended to contemporary illustrated broadsheets and emblem books. He probably owned some of these works himself, but in other cases he borrowed them from his more well-to-do acquaintances who showed an interest in his activities. His connection with the (emergent) world of the universities – the first university in the Northern Netherlands was founded in Leiden in 1575 – began only towards the end of his life, when he achieved recognition as an expert in his field and was consulted as such by renowned naturalists such as Rembert Dodonaeus from the University of Leiden.

For many of his descriptions of ordinary fish and natural phenomena, however, Coenen relied on first-hand observation close to home, practical experience and the exchange of information with others in the know in his immediate surroundings. As a boy, when he had been sent by his superiors to inspect creatures of the sea that had been washed up on the shore, he had acquired the habit of taking a notebook with him wherever he went to make notes on unusual fish, meteorological conditions and other experiences that were worth recording. Besides trading in fish, he dissected and dried them, bought unusual specimens and collected not only shells but also sayings and traditions about fishing and the sea. There were no limits on the time that he was willing to devote to his passionate interest, and he was prepared to go on long walks and even to spend considerable sums of money if necessary in order to collect information, see and, where possible, acquire unusual fish, pay artists to make sketches for him and consult publications. There is no evidence that he ever regarded travel as a necessary way to gain information. There was enough news right on his doorstep. He must have derived great pleasure from his life, his researches and the collecting of new knowledge. He liked a joke and a good meal. And he was fond of his familiar surroundings in the province of Holland.

Although the sea was a source of both income and knowledge, Coenen's own sea-faring experience was very limited and belonged to his youth (he may have sailed with the fishing boats that left Scheveningen for the northern tracts of the North Sea). When he did travel inland, it was mainly for business reasons, not in order to gain new information. However, as a man who was always eager for information about his sur-roundings, he could not but observe and note down many remarkable details during these travels. Some of these observations he later inserted in his manuscripts, such as remarks on the ways of preparing sturgeon and salmon in Flanders (aspects that were, of course, directly related to his business interests), and the unusual phenomenon of billions of may-flies covering the riverbanks, boats and passengers one day on a boat trip to the Southern Netherlands. Throughout his life he continued to investigate fish, collect unusual natural specimens and exchange information with fishers, traders and travellers.

An archival source detailing the day-to-day agenda of the Leiden local government gives us an intriguing glimpse into the activities of Coenen in later life. In September 1583 he put in a request to display both his *Fish Book* and his collection of dried fish at a commemora-tive civic fair for a small fee. This was not the first time that Coenen had displayed items from his collection for payment. As a young man, he had purchased a large squid (Dutch *poelomp*) on the fish market in Scheveningen

for two stuivers, taken it to his house in The Hague and the very same evening commis-sioned a painter to make a painting of it. Coenen's next step was to ask the permission of the authorities in The Hague to display the rare find for money. Not only was permission granted, but the authorities were themselves so interested in the affair that they called for the marine wonder to be brought to the city hall for them to admire it there.

Twenty years later, in 1566, Coenen obtained his second large squid in a similar way, buying it from a fisherman from Scheveningen who had come across it while fishing for shrimps. This time the event attracted even more interest, since this one turned out to have a political significance into the bargain. While the squid was at the painter's, rumour spread that it was a 'Beggar Fish' – an allusion to the Sea Beggars who were active in the Dutch revolt at the time. One of the symbols of the Sea Beggars was the beggar's purse – and Coenen's unusual squid turned out to have similar excrescences all over its tentacles. The painter's house was soon filled with a crowd, every member eager to procure a piece of the squid for himself. As Coenen wryly concludes: 'Thus this fish was sent to me to be displayed for money.'

Coenen's interests, both of a natural history and of a pecuniary kind, were thus clearly shared by many of his contemporaries. It would indeed be hard to imagine a better place than a market for the exhibition of the *Fish Book*, which, like all of Coenen's manuscripts, was itself a rambling collection bearing many resemblances to the 'cabinets of curiosities' that began to emerge in various

parts of Europe at precisely this time. It is therefore hardly surprising that many of the wonders of the sea described by Coenen featured in these Renaissance collections as well, in which shells, petrified snakes' or sharks' teeth, whale penises, coral, the sawfish or swordfish, and 'Jenny Hanivers' (dragon-like curios made from the dried bodies of skates and rays) regularly featured. In fact, the *Fish Book* was literally what many of the collections were figuratively considered to be: a book or theatre of the world.

The rise of the Renaissance *Kunst- und Wunderkammern*, as collections kept in cabinets of curiosities were called, was inex-tricably linked with the discovery of the New World on the eve of the sixteenth century. Ginger, cocoa, cloves, tomatoes and potatoes were in the first instance exotic products in European eyes. The tulip was first introduced to Europe in the sixteenth century, and coral from the tropical seas, preserved South American armadillos or dried crocodiles were sporadically available for those who could afford them. Many aristocratic or well-to-do collectors shared a passion for exotic plants, animals and other natural objects. One such was the very influential aristocrat Charles de Saint-Omer, who had a large collection in the Southern Netherlands. As the patron of the most famous European botanist of the six-teenth century, Carolus Clusius, Saint-Omer was jointly responsible for one of the largest and most splendid collections of plant illus-trations of the century (the *Libri Picturati A. 16-30*, now in the Jagiellon Library in Kraków). And it was the very same Saint-Omer with whom Coenen came into contact from 1560, thanks to his growing reputation on marine matters.

All the same, it would be misleading to make too strong a connection between Coenen and what were evidently collections of curiosities that belonged to an aristocratic milieu. One of the characteristics of the period spanned by Coenen's life is the astoundingly rapid upward social mobility of a new type of intellectual. The bold decision of an apothecary like Pierre Belon to write on the natural world in straightforward French rather than in convoluted Latin reflects a secular outlook that can be found in many of his contemporaries. His compatriot André Thevet, for instance, author of various works including a *Cosmographie universelle*, came from a similar background of apothecaries and barbersurgeons. Similar figures could be found in Switzerland, like the Platter family, or in Italy, like the Bolognese naturalist Ulisse Aldrovandi. The passion for the world of nature and the fascination with exotic plants and animals that came to Europe was clearly not confined to the narrow circles of a courtly elite. Recent studies on collections in various parts of Europe have shown that, alongside the renowned and grandiose collections of the Renaissance princes, more humble people were also building up what could at times be sizeable collections of objects of natural history in their shadow. Characteristic in this respect are Coenen's comments in the concluding pages of this manuscript on various kinds of inedible fish that were dried and sold as curiosities to apothecaries and 'city folk'. Coenen himself was no exception, because his manuscripts in fact formed part

of a larger collection of curiosities that included his dried turtle, swordfish (purchased from a fisherman in Scheveningen for a few rounds of beer), barnacle-goose, shark, exotic shells, and the unusual crab that he was given by a fisherman from Delfshaven who had nailed it above the door of his house – not to mention the live seal that lived in his house for a time! What makes Coenen so interesting in this connection is the fact that he managed to link his own observations to the information that could be gleaned from his friends in higher places and to record the combined results in text and image. In this respect, he might be seen to anticipate the type of person who could combine practical and theoretical knowledge, to whom Antonio Gramsci was later to refer as the 'organic intellectual'.

THE PRESENT EDITION

The work here presented as *The Whale Book* is the manuscript entitled 'Walvisboeck' that is in the library of the Royal Zoological Society in Antwerp (MS 30.021). It consists of a total of 125 folios (58 in Book 1, 66 in Book 2 and a fold-out sheet in between), 120 of which include one or more illustrations. The oblong folios originally measured 31 × 40 cm (the fold-out sheet measured 29 × 59 cm). They had been bound together in one volume at some time before their accession to the holdings of the Royal Zoological Society in 1843, and were restored and bound again in 1981. Five different watermarks appear on the various folios.

For decades the scarce reproductions of Coenen's illustrations that were to be found were almost totally confined to specialist

works on marine history. An exception is the Dutch-language biography of Adriaen Coenen by Florike Egmond published in 1997, which includes a number of colour illustrations, most of them taken from the pages of the *Fish Book*. The English summary included in that work, as well as a number of articles by the editors that appeared in international journals between 1994 and 2000, have served to raise interest in the man and his work. However, the present edition is the first of its kind to make Coenen's text and illustrations in colour available to a wide audience.

Although the examples referred to in this introduction are taken from both the *Fish Book* and *The Whale Book*, reproduction of the more than 500 folios of the two works is out of the question here. The present publication reproduces every illustrated page from the first volume of *The Whale Book*, a representative selection from the second volume and seven insets from the *Fish Book*. It is intended neither as a complete facsimile edition of *The Whale Book* nor as an academic edition. For that reason annotation and commentary have been reduced to a minimum. The editors have limited the selection of material to the most eye-catching and interesting illustrations from the folios of *The Whale Book* in order to make the vast majority of the material contained in a single work by Adriaen Coenen available to a wide audience. The accompanying texts have been translated from the Dutch, with the omission of certain features – such as nomenclature in different European languages and those passages in which Coenen simply copies from French or German works – to improve readability. The aim has been to convey as much as possible of Coenen's own style – witty, lively, full of anecdotes, personal and by no means literary. Where possible the rhyme scheme of his poems has been retained. Where there is a conventional translation for a Dutch word for a fish, the English equivalent is used and the Dutch word is indicated in parenthesis (e.g., 'Porpoise (*bruinvis*)'). In other cases, the Dutch term has been retained without any attempt at translation (e.g., *hil*). The units of measurement used by Coenen are: 1 foot (*voet*) = approximately 0.3 metres; 1 fathom (*vadem*) = 6 feet; 1 thumb (*duim*) = approximately 2.5 centimetres; 1 ell = approximately 69 centimetres. The editors are also responsible for the introduction, historical and textual comments, and suggestions for further reading.

xiv

FURTHER READING

Barthelmess, Klaus, and Joachim Münzing, *Monstrum Horrendum: Wale und Waldar-stellungen in der Druckgraphik des 16. Jahrhunderts und ihr motivkundlicher Einfluss*, Schriften des Deutschen Schif-fahrtsmuseums, vol. XIX (Hamburg, 1991)

Egmond, Florike, *Een bekende Scheveninger: Adriaen Coenen en zijn Visboeck van 1578* (Scheveningen, 1997) [with English summary]

—, and Peter Mason, 'Armadillos in Unlikely Places: Some Unpublished Sixteenth-Century Sources for New World Rezeptionsgeschichte in Northern Europe', *Ibero-Amerikanisches Archiv. Zeitschrift für Sozialwissenschaften und Geschichte*, XX/1–2 (1994), pp. 3–52

—, 'Report on a Wild Goose Chase', *Journal of the History of Collections*, VII/1 (1995), pp. 25–43

—, 'Een portret van Coenraet van Schilperoort (1577–1636)', *Bulletin van het Rijksmuseum*, XLIII/1 (1995), pp. 36–58

—, 'Skeletons on Show: Learned Entertainment and Popular Knowledge', *History Workshop*, XL (1996), pp. 92–116 [with English summary]

—, 'Excursions', Chapter 1 of their *The Mammoth and the Mouse: Microhistory and Morphology* (Baltimore and London, 1997), pp. 7–36

—, '"These Are People Who Eat Raw Fish": Contours of the Ethnographic Imagination in the Sixteenth Century', *Viator: Medieval and Renaissance Studies*, XXXI (2000), pp. 311–60

ACKNOWLEDGEMENTS

This publication commemorates the contribution to whale conservation of Ferdinand von der Assen, commissioner for the Netherlands in the International Whaling Commission for twenty years.

We are most grateful to Fernand Schrevens of the Royal Zoological Society of Antwerp for his invaluable assistance in the gestation and implementation of this project over the years, and to the Society itself for kindly granting permission to reproduce one of its most precious holdings.

We also owe a great debt of gratitude to Hans Nieuwerhuis, a fellow villager of Adriaen Coenen, for his moral and technical support for the Coenen project from its very inception. Like a modern Adriaen Coenen, the marine biologist Kees Lankester, who has years of experience in the field of whaling and fisheries, has added up-to-date information about the creatures illustrated by Coenen, including the modern scientific name, a description of physical appearance, habitat, behaviour or other aspects on which biological research has been conducted, and anecdotes or particular features where appropriate. He received advice from Vassili Papastavrou and Klaus Barthelmess.

Maudy Marcus conducted the investigation of the physical state of the manuscript. She would also like to thank Saskia van Bergen for technical advice.

The photographs and digitization are the work of Dries van den Brande.

Finally, it has been a pleasure to work again with the capable team at Reaktion Books.

The First Book

DAT · EERSTE · BOOCK ·

Van menich derley Was visschin
Ende Ander seltene groote
Vbonderlyke visschin ·

Bottlenose whale

On 18 August 1584 a wondrous fish was washed up on the island of Schouwen one and a half miles from Zierikzee. The Scheveningen fishers call it a *hil* and say that a *hil* has a pointed snout like a porpoise. This one was 28 feet long, 16 feet in diameter, his snout was 2 feet long, and his forehead 2 feet 8 thumbs high and 1 foot 7 thumbs wide at the tip. There was a hole above his eye from which he expels water. The dorsal fin was 2 feet 3 thumbs long and one and a half feet wide; the side fin was 2.5 feet long; his penis 1.5 feet 5 thumbs long. His back was pinkish in colour with some light grey under the belly, but he had no teeth in his mouth. His fins were blackish.

This illustration was sent with this inscription from Zeeland to Doctor Dodonaeus who teaches medicine in Leiden at the university and used to be personal physician to the emperor. I received this illustration from him and have painted this plate and the corresponding text after it.

Rembert Dodoens (1516/17–1585) was a world-famous zoologist and botanist. He was physician in ordinary to the Holy Roman Emperor Maximilian II and his successor, Rudolf II, in Vienna between 1574 and 1577. He was Professor of Medicine at the University of Leiden at the time of his death in 1585.

According to Coenen, *hil* is a generic term for whales and dolphins. He also confuses porpoises with dolphins several times in the text. The description, dimensions and illustration come closest to a Northern bottlenose whale (*Hyperoodon ampullatus*). The proportions in this plate are not entirely correct, but the shape, size and colour are characteristic. What Coenen calls 'pinkish' in the text is a brownish red in the illustration. The only larger whale of this colour is the bottlenose whale, which is chocolate brown with light-brown flanks.

The bottlenose whale is a toothed whale that can grow to a length of 10 metres. It lives mainly on squid and is an excellent diver. During a recent experiment involving two tagged whales near Nova Scotia in Canada, a maximal depth of 1,485 metres was recorded, and they were able to stay under water for 70 minutes without a break. Although a whale of the high seas, the bottlenose whale is occasionally seen in the shallow waters of the North Sea. The last bottlenose whale to be sighted off the Dutch coast was in 1997, when one of them swam around for a few days in Zierikzee harbour – the exact spot where the whale described by Coenen was seen in 1584. Both sightings were media items.

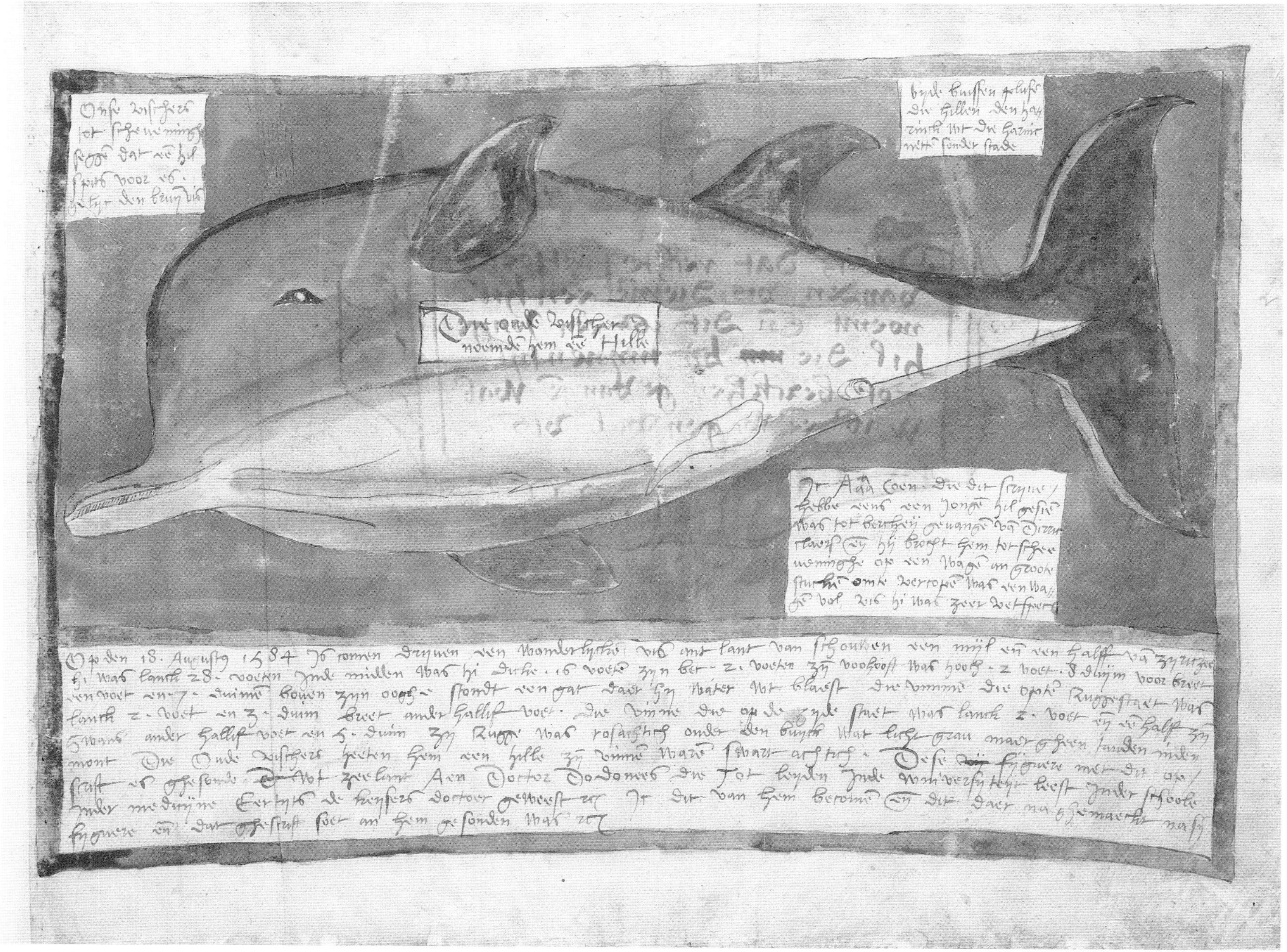
Op den 18. Augusty 1584

This is an illustration of the fish called a *hil*

The *hil* is classified as one of the big whales among us. In some countries big porpoises are called dolphins, but we call them *hillen*. That is why some represent the dolphin like this and in some countries they call our porpoises young dolphins.

The fishers on our boats say that *hillen* are big fish, almost as big as whales, but that they differ from them because they do not spout water out of pipes on their head or from their nostrils. These *hillen* have a sharply pointed snout, as can be seen here.

In my youth, around 1534, a young *hil* like this one was caught in Berckheji. I, Adriaen Coenen, who write this have seen that young *hil*. The man who caught him carried him on a cart to Scheveningen to sell in large pieces. It certainly was a cartload of fish; it was very oily speck. The train-oil was very good for bruised and broken limbs, and it didn't taste bad.

Around the same time a big fish was stranded on the coast opposite Den Briel. My master sent me there with axes and knives to cut pieces off it, but when we arrived we were told that it had been driven to Den Briel on the other side by a storm. Long afterwards, 5 or 6 years, I happened to be near Rockanje to look for a ship I had business with, and when I got there I saw a large piece of this big fish still lying on the shore. It was so big I could stand on it, like on the side of a fishing boat. It had been a terribly big fish, the marine receiver at Rockanje told me, who had extracted a lot of train-oil from it and sold it for a high price; he said that it was a *hil*.

The 'master' is the supervisor of the Scheveningen fish auction under whom the young Coenen was learning the trade. Independent sources confirm the storm of late 1534, when more than 40 ships, mainly herring boats, were wrecked. Rockanje and Den Briel (modern Brielle) are both in Voorne facing the Hook of Holland.

Coenen's recordings of the strandings of 1534 and *circa* 1540 are among the earliest documented accounts of strandings in the Netherlands. The most likely *hil* to be described here is a bottlenose dolphin (*Tursiops truncatus*), which has a long snout.

Whales and dolphins breathe through a blowhole situated on the top of the head. The moist air is forced out of the lungs under great pressure and fresh air is rapidly inhaled. Large whales produce a blow that is visible like a fountain. Whales can also be seen blowing when the temperature is high. The blow is actually condensation of the air from the lungs that is produced by the sudden change in pressure, not in temperature. The change in pressure in the case of dolphins is apparently not enough to make their blow visible. Some types of whale can be identified by their blow. The blue whale has a narrow blow that can reach a height of 9 metres. The bowhead whale and the right whale have a double blow. The sperm whale has its blowhole left of centre, but its blow shoots forwards.

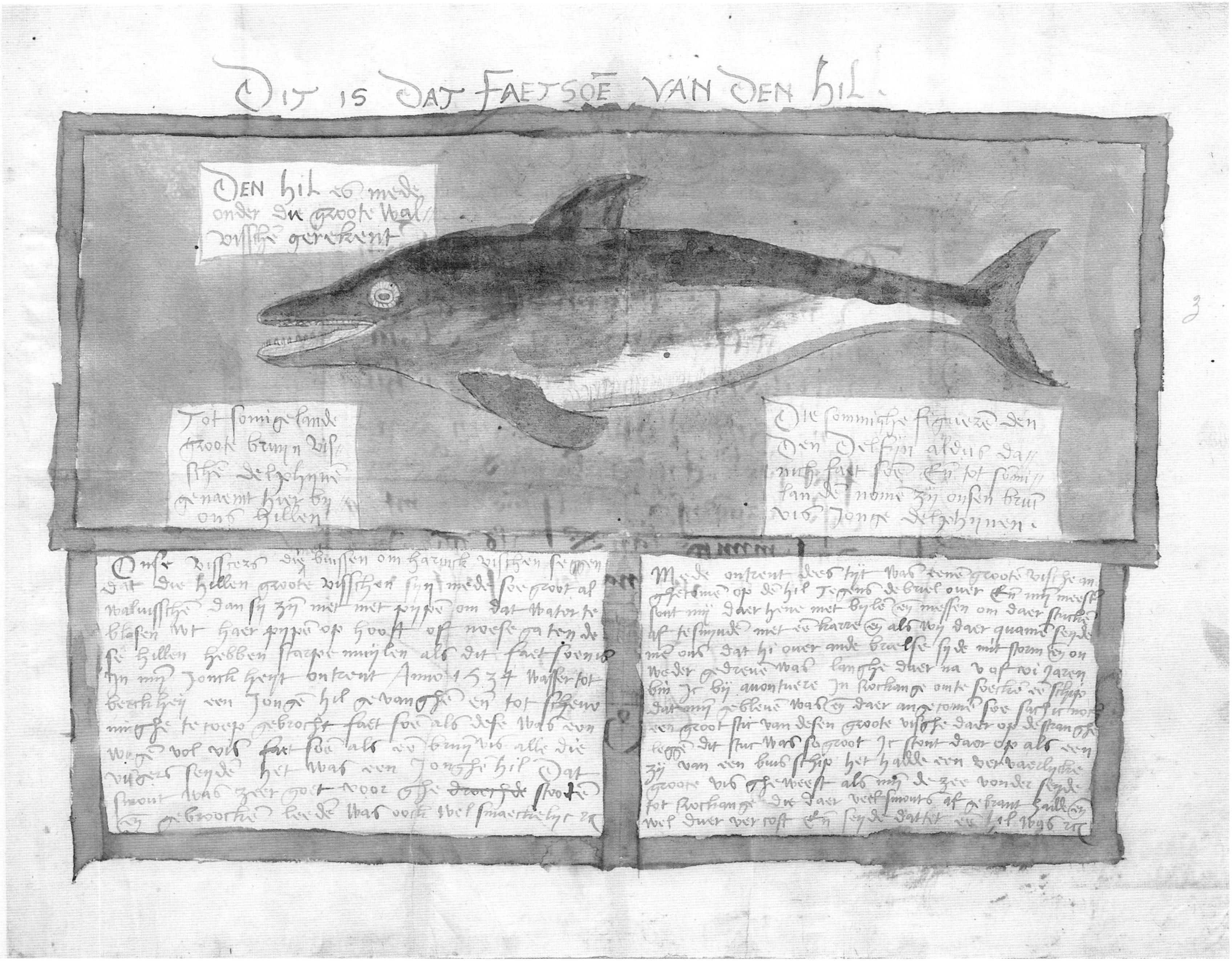
Dit is dat faetsoe van den hil

This is a good illustration of our porpoises

The female with young and the male.

People say that when the porpoises are big they are *hillen*, because they look identical. I have noticed that in some countries people call our porpoises dolphins, about which more in this book.

Pierre Belon gives these names: *orca* and *ouldre* or *grand marsouin*. In Holland we call them *bruinvis* or *meerzwijn*. I who write this have once cut open a porpoise and removed the young, that was 3.5 feet long. The mother was 7 feet long. Ordinary porpoises are 5 to 6 feet long, the largest 7 feet. The first I saw weighed a hundred pounds. The females are usually the heaviest and the largest. Those porpoises are highly appreciated as food during Lent by the rich canons in Maastricht, Liège and Aachen. They are also very keen on porpoises in London in England. When the fishers from here in Holland sail to England with plaice or haddock, depending on the season, and they manage to catch a porpoise or seal, they take it with them to England. It first has to be presented to the queen, and she usually keeps it and pays for it so that the merchant does not suffer a loss.

These porpoises are caught here in Holland by the fishers who use nets to catch cod, and those who catch salmon in nets also catch them in their nets sometimes. But I who write this, Adriaen Coenen, fish auctioneer in Scheveningen, have never heard that they were caught on hooks except once. When I was auctioning the fish in Scheveningen, a fisher from Zeeland told me – when he came with his fish and while we were discussing all kinds of things concerning fish – that he had once caught a porpoise on a hook, and once a sturgeon too. The crew of his boat confirmed that it was true. We in Scheveningen considered that this was something new and rare because it had never happened to us.

The porpoise on the left who is depicted after giving birth goes back to one of the 21 wood-cuts from the earliest work on fish by the French naturalist and traveller Pierre Belon (1517–1564/5). *Histoire naturelle des étranges poissons marins*, which was published in Paris in 1551. Since Belon mentions a collection of drawings of fish compiled by Guillaume Rondelet, whose *De piscibus marinis* of 1554 contains a very similar illustration, it seems likely that the woodcuts by both Belon and Rondelet go back to this common source.

The harbour porpoise (*Phocoena phocoena*) was common on the Dutch coast in Coenen's days and his description of it is accurate. They are usually between 1.5 and 1.8 metres long but can grow to a length of more than 2 metres. The females are the largest and heaviest. The largest known baby harbour porpoise at birth in recent observations was 90 centimetres long.

Many porpoises fall victim to fisheries. Particularly when nylon gill-nets are used, fishermen have many so-called by-catches of dolphins and porpoises that drown in their nets. For the North Sea the minimal by-catch is estimated at 7,000 porpoises a year.

Whales found in British waters are formally the property of the Crown by a statute of 1324, when the term 'Fishes Royal' was introduced. This status was confirmed by Parliament in 1970.

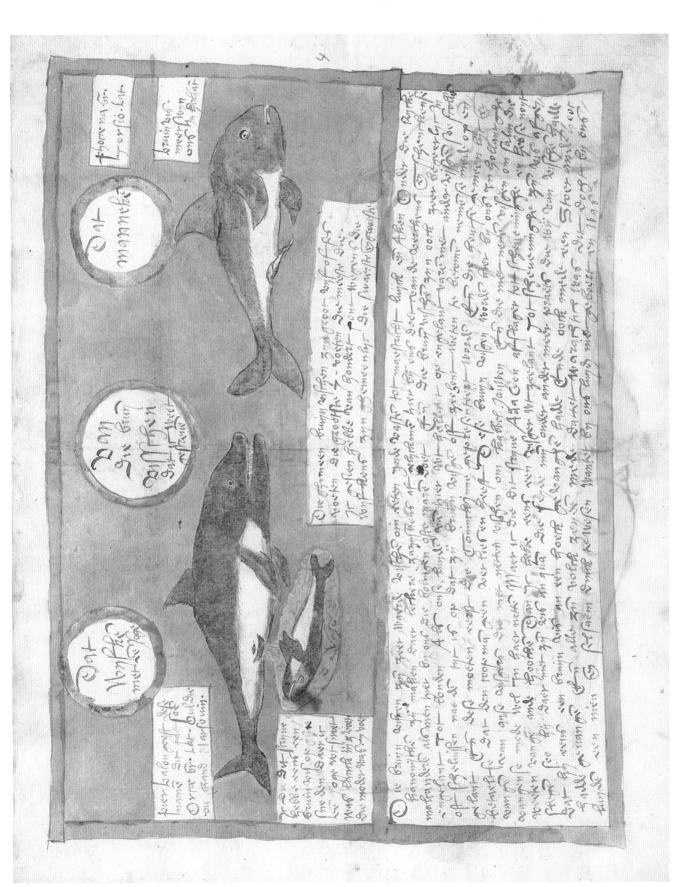

Sperm whale (*potvis*)

A potswal, called a potshooft by our fishers. This is one of the three fish that were stranded near the village of Westerheij on 23 November 1577. They were remarkably big fish, all three male, and the same in appearance. They were lying about a broadside from one another on the beach when I saw them there. The largest was 55 feet, the second 49 feet, the third 48 feet.

All three fish were black, the whole body as fat as a porpoise, but somewhat less fatty or oily in proportion to their size, and with rather more meat. They had short teeth in the lower jaws, which protruded like the horns of a young cow, and there were holes in the upper jaws into which the teeth fitted. They had small eyes considering their size, smaller than the eyes of a cow. All three had sheaths near the belly that were tapered like a bull's pizzle, and a very blunt head. Together these three fish raised 578 guilders, of which 12 guilders were given to the poor.

Westerheij was the place of birth of Coenen's mother, Dirkje Adriaensdr van Schilperoort. Coenen illustrated this sperm whale in each of his three extant manuscripts. The three beached sperm whales of November 1577, part of a group of thirteen, are also illustrated in a contemporary pamphlet printed in Antwerp by Willem van Haecht with an engraving designed by Johann Wierix.

EEN·POTS·VAL.

EEN·Wal·

Anno 1577

Whale (*walvis*)

True-to-life portrait and dimensions of the fish caught on 2 July 1577. In the year of Our Lord 1577, on the day of 2 July, a living fish was caught between Haeften and Saaftinge in the river Schelde near Antwerp close to the dyke. It could not float there because the water was too shallow. It was finished off with picks, hooks and other instruments. It roared in a terrible fashion and made an enormous hullabaloo before it died, so that the water was tremendously stirred up, churned up and troubled from bottom to top. Afterwards it was dragged with ropes and small boats to Haeften.

Its skin had no scales and was like leather, as grey as lead. He was 58 feet long, 16 feet 3 thumbs high, and 12 feet broad. The distance from the tip of his mouth to the farthest point of his eyes was 15 feet, and 4 feet 3 thumbs from the eyes to the fin. The fins were 5 feet 2 thumbs long. He had 50 teeth in the lower jaw and there were 50 holes in the upper jaw into which the teeth fitted. His jaw was 7 thumbs wide at the tip, but 1 foot 6 thumbs at the back, with a length of 8 feet. The tongue lay in the throat like a liver and was the size of a barrel of beer. The tail was 14 feet 3 thumbs wide. And his penis was 8 feet long and tapering. Above his nose he had an opening or split, from which he spouted excess water. The boat-men who killed him called him a whale and said that there were two others dead near Bieselinge.

Coenen's watercolour is based on an engraving by Pieter Baltens for a pamphlet printed by Gerard Smits in Antwerp. His text is based on the trilingual text of that pamphlet by the local physician Hugo Favolius.

The sperm whale (*Physeter macrocephalus*) was called a *potswis* (compare the modern German *pottwal*) in Coenen's day. It can dive to great depths and remain underwater for a long time. It feeds on squid and fish that it finds by echolocation. Adult male sperm whales have harems. Groups of young females and young male sperm whales are found in various locations near the coastline, especially in the tropics. The big males, which can grow up to 1.5 times the size of a fully grown female, lead mostly solitary lives, migrating to cold waters in higher latitudes.

Baleen whale (*balena*)

This is a big whale that is called *belua* or *balena* as described below. Our fishers here give all rare big fish the following names in Dutch: a. *walvissen*, b. *wilde belijen*, c. *hillen*, d. *westerlingen*, e. *potshoofden*. The *hillen* have pointed heads, the *potshoofden* (sperm whales) have blunt heads, and the whales (*walvissen*) have pipes above the head from which they spout water.

The baleen whale is a very large beast in the sea and spouts a lot of water as if it were a cloud, which sometimes causes ships considerable trouble. The baleen whale is not seen until the winter comes. In the summer it is rarely seen; they lie hidden in their sweet meadows and that is where they give birth. And when they give birth they are in such pain that they come to the surface for help. They give birth just like the other large animals of the earth and sleep too. If a storm is brewing they shelter their young in their jaws and blow them out again once the storm is over. They reach adult length in two years.

The baleen whale is an extremely large fish that stirs up the sea with big waves and billows that come from the sea bed. They are a great danger to ships, as happened with the ships of Alexander the Great. There are many of this kind of fish in the Eastern Sea.

Balata is a beast of the sea and behaves contrary to nature compared with other animals, because when she feels the young in her belly she pulls them out. If they are fully grown she leaves them outside, but if they are still too small she puts them back in the belly to grow fully.

Although the resemblance in the painting is not very close, several of the features mentioned by Coenen could refer to the bowhead whale (*Balaena mysticetus*). Coenen refers to a large, round whale with a double blow that is seen only in winter (bowhead whales normally spend the summer in Arctic waters). However, the bowhead whale is a baleen whale, not a toothed whale. The baleen or whalebone refers to the keratin (horn) plates that are found in large whales instead of teeth. They use them to filter the water through the baleens, after which their food (small fish and zooplankton) is left behind in their mouth.

Coenen lived a few decades before the English and Dutch discovered that many bowhead whales were to be found near Spitsbergen. They were regarded as a good source of oil for lamps. The large-scale commercial hunting of the bowhead whale began in 1611. They are considered virtually extinct in the east Atlantic, but there are still occasional confirmed sightings (there were ten between 1990 and 2000).

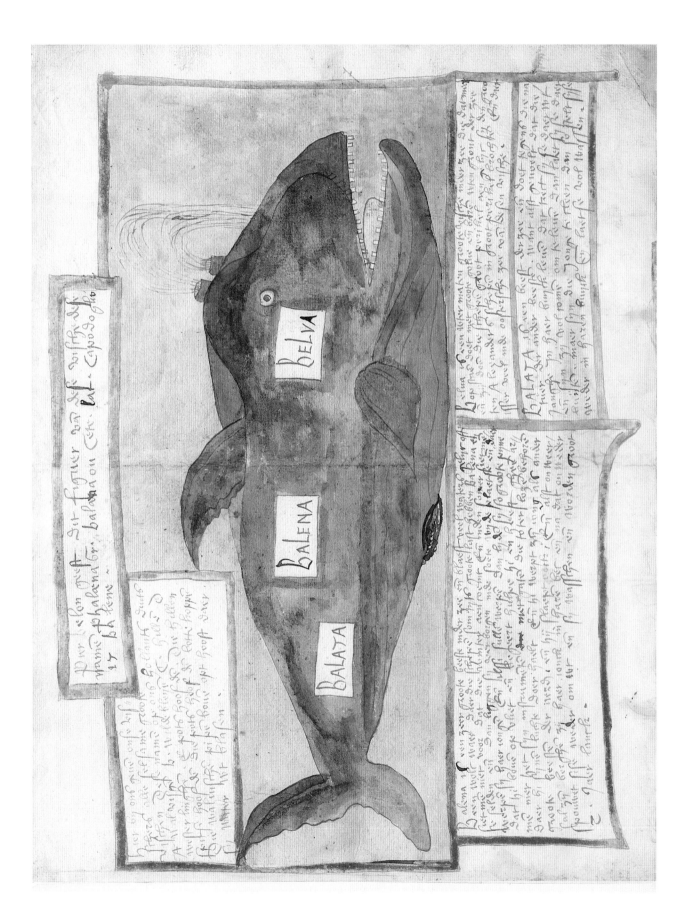

About the struggle between the whale and the orca

Olaus Magnus describes the struggle between the whale and the orca in his 21st book. Although the whale is so big – for instance, 100 or 300 feet long and with a tough, thick body – it has an enemy in the orca, which is much smaller but also much bolder and crueller, both in jumping and in attacking. The orca looks like a ship turned upside down and has awfully sharp teeth with which it cuts open and tears the belly of the whale. Or it stabs the whale with the sharp fin on its back, by swimming again and again under the whale and tormenting it so long in this way that the whale is forced to flee to the depths of the sea or to seek refuge in shallow water or on dry land. Because its body is so heavy, the whale cannot manoeuvre easily and does not know how to defend itself against the tricks of the orca, but flees straight away, although this does not really help because the whale is a slow swimmer and because of the great weight it is burdened with. So it really ought to have a pilot in the depths of the sea to evade such grave dangers.

Olaf Stor (1490–1558), latinized as Olaus Magnus, Archbishop of Uppsala, spent the last fifteen years of his life in Rome, where in 1555 he published an illustrated history of the Scandinavian countries, *Historia de gentibus septentrionalibus, . . . necnon universis pene animalibus in Septentrione degentibus*. The last three books were dedicated to fish, monstrous fish and insects. Coenen is probably drawing on the images and texts from Olaus Magnus that were incorporated in Conrad Gessner's vast and methodical compilation on natural history in several volumes. Gessner (1516–1565) was a Swiss physician and professor of Greek and Latin.

Up to 9 metres in length and with large teeth, the orca (*Orcinus orca*) is the largest predator in the world. It usually feeds on fish, but also eats seals and whales. Olaus is right in stating that the whale is no match for the orca. They hunt in a group that wears the prey out.

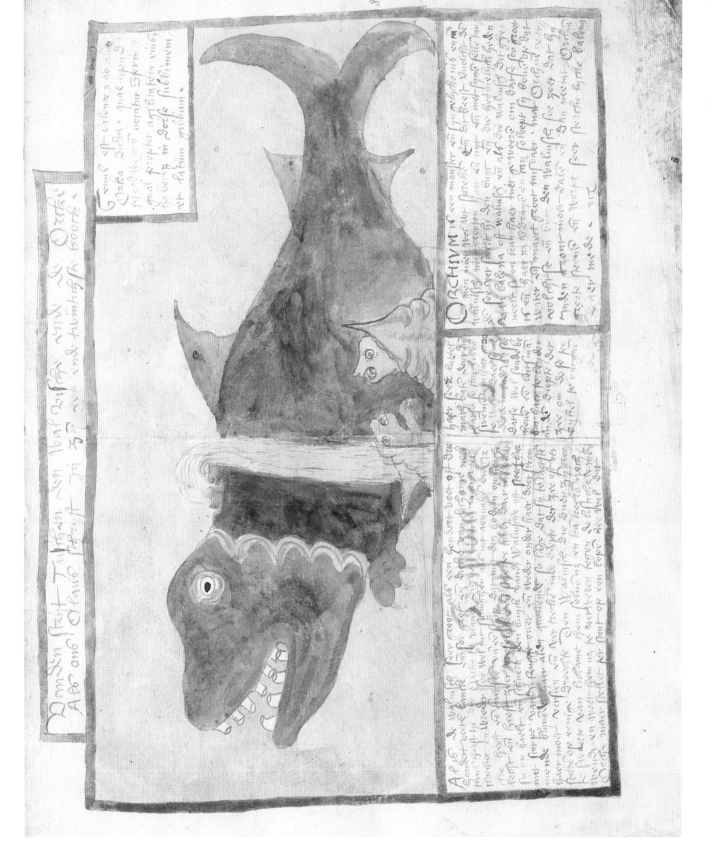

Marine monsters

The seamen didn't know it was an island
Read the text below and you'll understand.

Awesome marine monsters off the coast of Norway (as Olaus Magnus describes). *Aspidochelon phisiologus* is a large *belua* in the sea and a big whale. His skin is very rough and he often floats with his back high above the water. The outer layer of the skin of this whale looks like sand from sand dunes, so that it often happens that the seamen who see him think that it is an island. And when the seamen come close, then they row up to him with a small boat, moor, and make a fire to cook their food. When the whale feels the heat of the fire, he swims away, the people are drowned, and he pulls the boats underwater. When this whale is hungry he opens his mouth and exhales a sweet-smelling vapour so that the smaller fish smell it and are attracted by it. When his mouth is full he swallows them all in one gulp. That is how he gathers his food. This is how Olaus describes it.

Coenen often enlivens his albums with rhymes like these of his own making. Rhyming was an activity practised by both elite and more humble circles in his day. The *aspidochelone* appears as a sea turtle in the *Physiologus*, a natural history compilation put together in Alexandria in the second century AD, so-called because most of the chapters contain the phrase 'the Physiologus says . . .'. It is known from a Latin manuscript of the eighth or ninth century and later. In medieval bestiaries the *aspidochelone* became a fish. Although Coenen quotes Olaus as his source, the same information about being mistaken for an island and about the use of its sweet breath as a lure can already be found in bestiaries.

Sperm whale (*potvis*)

This fish was stranded on 11 March 1566. A wondrous fish seen between Zandvoort and House Brederode on the beach with a length measuring 42 feet. He was 35 feet wide. He kept swimming for a while until he got stuck and kept spouting barrelfuls of water from his nostrils.

Coenen illustrated this sperm whale in all three of his extant manuscripts. Here he illustrates it twice: once in the water and once on land.

The sperm whale was intensively hunted in the nineteenth and twentieth centuries. The oil contained in the head of the sperm whale, spermaceti, provides a highly refined grease. The hunting of sperm whales has concentrated on the males in the cold waters near the North Pole and South Pole since the 1950s. These are the dominant males in the harem system of sperm whales. Commercial sperm whale hunting was formally halted in 1981. Today living sperm whales have proved to be of much greater economic value and (sperm) whale-watching has become a major tourist industry.

A marine serpent (*zeeslang*)

A great and wondrous marine serpent; when it appears, something wondrous happens, just as after the appearance of a comet, as Olaus Magnus describes in his 21st book.

All those who traverse the Norwegian waters, whether to fish or for trade, say that the Norwegian serpent is a very terrible thing. It is more than 200 feet long and 20 wide and usually lurks near rocks and caves beside the coast near Bergen in Norway. This serpent only leaves its cave on summer nights when the weather is very good to eat calves, lambs and pigs, or it swims further out to sea to eat cuttlefish, sea crabs and other creatures. The serpent has hanging hair and very sharp scales, is black in colour and has keen, brightly coloured eyes. This serpent is very dangerous and destructive for the ships, because it can rise high out of the water like a column and then drags the people out of the ships and eats them. This is a great evil for the kingdom of Norway, because if it appears there is always a major change imminent, such as the death or banishment of a king or a war.

There is also a wondrously large serpent in the island of Moos in the diocese of Hammeren. If it appears, a change is on the way in the kingdom of Norway, just as elsewhere in the world such a change is heralded by the appearance of a comet. In 1522 this serpent was seen rising high out of the water. Through long observation it was determined that this serpent was 50 cubits long. Immediately afterwards the king was banished and the priests and prelates were persecuted. This is what Olaus Magnus describes.

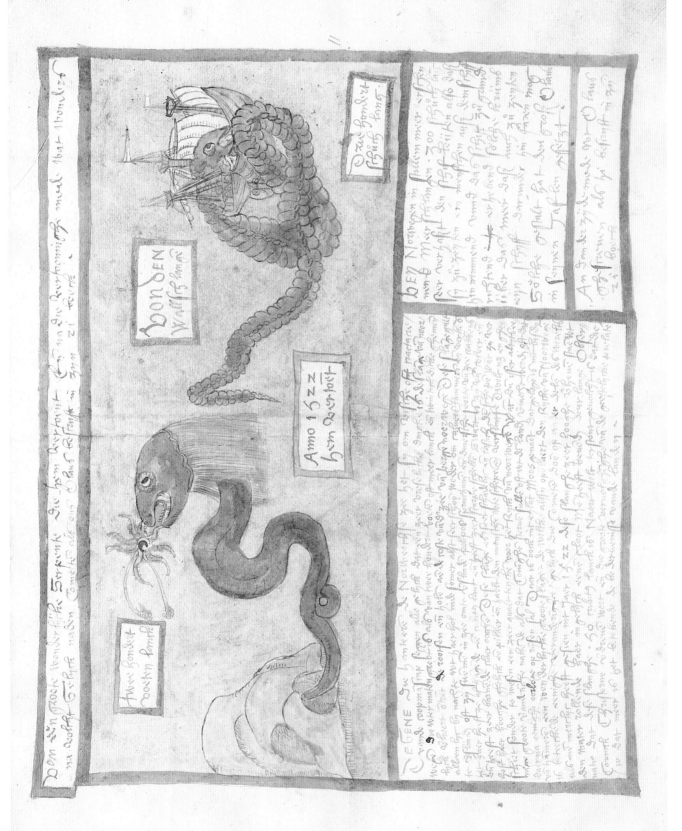

A long and very slender eel (*zeeworm*)

Olaus describes it in his 21st book. This eel is 40 feet long. It resembles our conger eel. There is an eel off the Norwegian coast, greyish-blue in colour, that is 40 cubits or more long, but barely as thick as a small child's arm. It swims so stealthily through the water that it is barely possible to see movement where it has been swimming. This eel does not bother anyone and does no harm, except when it is touched by human hands, because the contact with its thin skin causes the fingers to swell. When the eel is gripped and hurt by lobsters, it tries to escape by wriggling, but that is in vain, because lobsters have sharp claws like pincers and clutch the eel so tightly that it is anchored, as it were. I have seen this eel but never touched it because the seamen had warned me of the danger. That is what Olaus writes about the eel. Aristotle and Pliny have also written about eels.

The eel on the right is clearly copied from Pierre Belon's *De aquatilibus, libri duo* (1553), which was published in French two years later as *La nature et diversité des poissons.*

These marine serpents are enormous. However, the conger eel (*Conger conger*) mentioned by Coenen can only grow to a maximum of 3 metres or so in length. The conger eel is a large relative of the common eel, but it spends the whole of its life in the ocean between the Azores and Gibraltar and does not thrive in fresh water. The other marine serpent described by Coenen could be the long-jawed snake eel (*Ophisurus serpens*), which can reach a length of 2.5 metres.

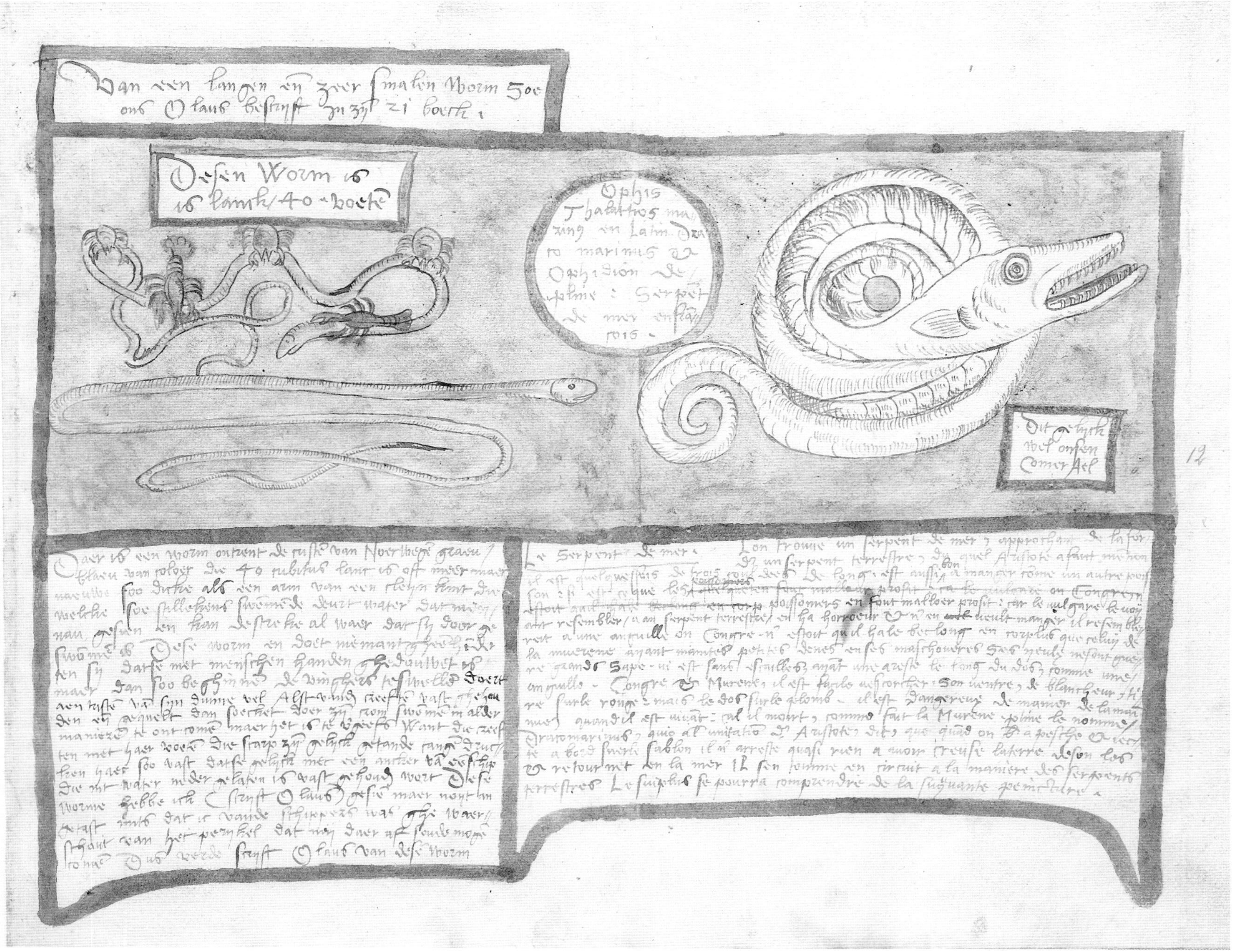
Van een langen en zeer smalen Worm soo ons Olaus beschryft in zyn 21 boeck.
Desen Worm is is lanck 40 voet
Ophis Thalattios

Two strange fish

Left-hand fish: Scolopendra cetaeca, a *Walmassel*. A creature like this is supposed to have been seen in India, and is described by Aelian.

Right-hand fish: A fish with three gold teeth, found in Ireland. Olaus illustrates this fish but does not give it a name. It is supposed to be enormous in size with strong, long, sharp teeth.

Aelian (Claudius Aelianus), a writer of the second century AD who taught rhetoric in Rome, was the author of *De natura animalium* (*On the Characteristics of Animals*), one of the most influential works of natural history from antiquity. The facts it contains were gleaned from earlier and contemporary Greek writers; not a single Latin writer is mentioned. It was first translated from Greek into Latin in 1533 by Pierre Gilles. The sea-scolopendra is called the biggest of the sea monsters in XIII.23.

Note Coenen's use of the rider 'is supposed to be' to introduce a note of caution; Conrad Gessner, who named the second of these creatures *aper* because of its boar-like appearance, had already expressed his reservations about the genuineness of these marine marvels.

The name given by Coenen allows a comparison with the centipedes *Scolopendridae*, with the genus *Scolopendra*. The creature in Coenen's drawing is indeed similar to the centipede *Scolopendra heros*.

There are centipedes in the North Sea, clam worms. The large or green clam worm can be 40 centimetres long. Its favourite habitat is underneath banks of shells. The body is green on top, with an iridescent pink belly. On one night of the year, at full moon in April, the green clam worms emerge from the depths and swim to the surface to mate. The common marine centipede, a smaller clam worm about 20 centimetres long (*Nereis diversicolor*), is mainly found in tidal areas. It occurs in a variety of colours – red, green, yellow and brown – hence its scientific name.

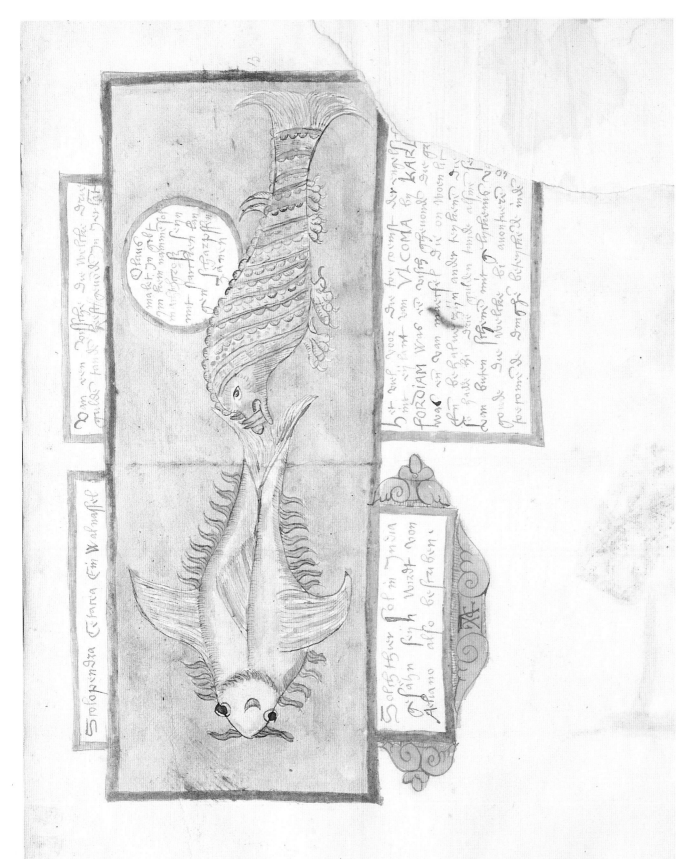

25

Sunfish (*maanvis*)

This is an illustration of a fish caught on 14 October 1583 behind England by Willemaertens and Dingeman Temanszoon, fishermen from Zierikzee. He was 1.5 feet 4.5 thumbs long, the large fins 9 thumbs, the frontal fins 3 thumbs. The depth 1 foot 4 thumbs. His belly was like silver without scales. I have drawn this portrait from an illustration which was sent to Doctor Dodoens who teaches medicine at the University of Leiden. Gessner describes this fish and calls it the *maanvis*.

This fish is unknown to the fishers of Scheveningen, and none of them knows its name, but a fisher who was fishing for herrings in his boat caught one and sent it to me, Adriaen Coenen, as I have described in more detail in my *Big Fish Book*. The captain of that ship came from Scheveningen and was called Cornelis Gerits Piers Imme Jostenman. This fish was dried while it was still on board. I kept it for a long time in my house. Afterwards I sold it to an adventurer in 1560.

Moreover, a fish like this was washed up dead on the coast about half a mile from our village of Scheveningen on 12 December 1565. This one was very big, 8 feet long and 6 feet high. When it had been disembowelled, I had it put in a cart, and 8 sturdy seamen had their hands full with it. I intended to dry the skin with the head, but because it was wet winter weather the beast rotted completely. I had a portrait made of the fish and gave the portrait to the Lord of Oosterwijk and President Mr Cornelis Suys, who were very surprised by it, and considered that after its appearance something wondrous would happen, and that is what happened.

The Swiss physician and professor of Greek and Latin Conrad Gessner (1516–1565) produced a vast and methodical compilation on natural history in several volumes. The volume on fish was first published in 1558. Coenen knew it through the German translation by Cunrat Forer.

Cornelis Suys (1514–1580), knight and Lord of Rijswijk, was a very high-ranking civil servant in the service of the Habsburg administration of the Netherlands. He studied in Orléans and was President of the Provincial Court of Holland from 1559 to 1572. During the Dutch Revolt he continued to support the Habsburgs, which explains why he had to flee to the Southern Netherlands in 1579. During this turbulent period he regularly lent Adriaen Coenen books on ichthyology. Coenen was a regular guest at his table.

Splinter van Hargen, nobleman and Lord of Oosterwijk, was a relative of Cornelis Suys. He also supported Habsburg rule and had to leave for the Southern Netherlands. Both men were friends of Janus Secundus, an early sixteenth-century Latin poet in Holland.

Coenen provides a very naturalistic image of the sunfish (*Mola mola*), which is occasionally found in the North Sea. The exemplar described by Coenen was a very big one. The sunfish is the heaviest of the bony fish. A gigantic exemplar found off the coast of Australia was more than 3 metres high and 2.5 metres long. Despite its size, the sunfish lives on small fry such as plankton, jellyfish and small crustaceans. They sometimes float in groups on the surface and allow sea birds to eat the parasites off their skin.

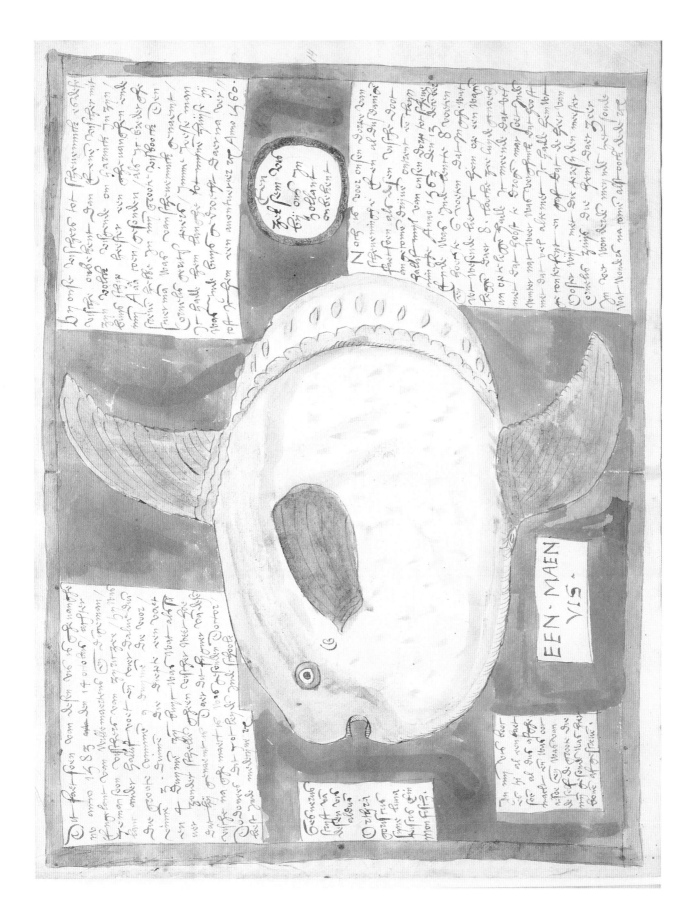

EEN · MAEN
· VIS ·

Certificate from Gibraltar of a wondrous tunny, May 1565

I, Johan Frutuoso, royal notary, a resident of this noble city of Gibraltar, attest and witness to all who shall see this that it is the truth. Certain information has been given to me, the notary of the court of law of this city, by six witnesses clearly indicating that 15 or 16 days ago a tunny was found on the coast of the sea in the city of Ceuta on which are painted, as it were, many galleys, masts, oars, rowers, artillery and more vessels and an armed galliot which appeared to want to storm one another. This was all done in a very natural and realistic manner as if a drawing had been made in the skin and flesh of this tunny in a wondrous way, never seen before. Done in Gibraltar, 13 May 1565, and below I have set my signature as a witness to its truth, signed Johan Frutuoso.

Tunnies are very tasty fish, with a delicate flavour. They are rarely caught here on the coast of Holland.

Coenen's source is a pamphlet with a wood-cut engraving by Matthäus Franck from 1565. Ceuta is a Spanish enclave on the North African coast opposite Gibraltar.

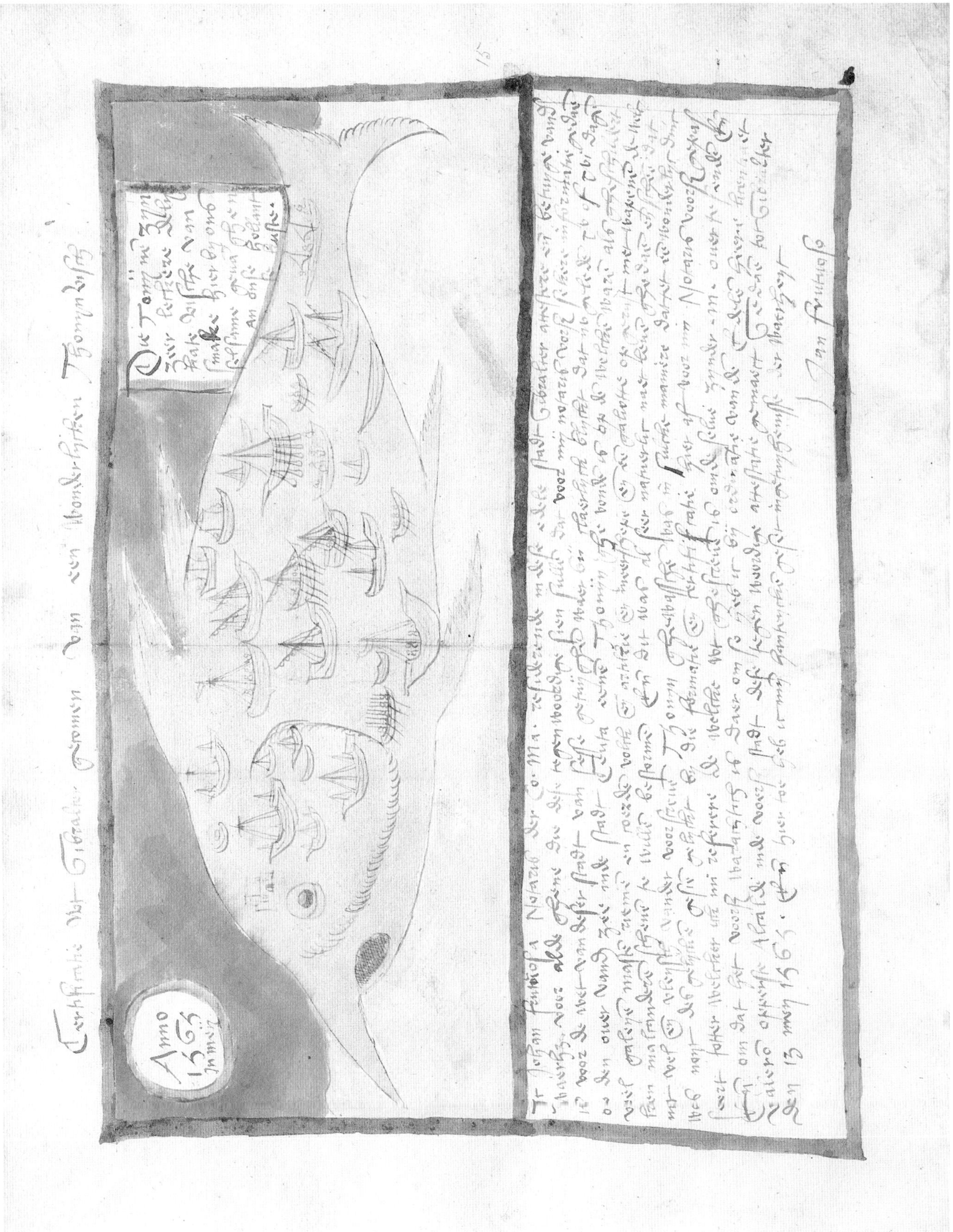
Anno 1563

Three fish that I, Adriaen Coenen, have seen and that are called tunnies

Tunnies are unknown to the fishers on the Dutch coast; they are very tasty. These fish have small scales on their head, are as slippery as the salmon, and look like the mackerel.

On 18 July 1545 – it was a Saturday – a fishmonger came from Westerheij to the fish market in The Hague. He had a fish with him that looked like the first of these three fish to sell it here, but people didn't know this fish, so he couldn't sell it. So he had a piece of it cooked and gave the people a taste. Then he did sell some, and he gave me a piece as a present. It was a very tasty fish, reddish like salmon, and just as oily, appetizing and full of flavour. When the people had all tasted it, he could have sold much more if he had had more fish. He told me that this fish weighed a hundred pounds. Some people said that it was a tunny and some said that the tunny is oily. A pastrycook who knew something about them said that this fish is called *poervis* as well as tunny in France, but that it is unknown to the fishers of Scheveningen.

The second one I saw was in the house of Mr Kabau, the steward of the Esparge, a son of Mr Vinsent. He told me to come to The Hague to see this fish (since I wrote a lot about fish) and so that I could tell him what kind of a fish it was. This one was a big fish, another tunny, weighing more than a hundred pounds. We talked a lot about fish over dinner, because I stayed at his place for a meal. He gave many good friends each a piece of this tunny.

The third one I saw was in our village of Scheveningen. Three or four fishermen had found it on the beach and asked me what kind of a fish it was, because they didn't recognize it. They divided it between them and gave me a piece too. So that's how I've come to see three of them. They are unknown here on the Dutch coast, and they are rarely caught by our fishermen. They are found more often in other seas, as I have described in my *Big Fish Book*. I wrote this in October 1584.

Jacob van Mierop, Lord of Kabau, was officially entitled – after some deductions – to what the sea washed up. Mr Vinsent is Vincent Cornelisz van Mierop, who held estates in Holland. He was a high-ranking civil servant (Master of the Auditor's Office) and, as clerk of the register of the Counts of Holland, a predecessor of Cornelis Suys from 1518 to 1550.

These fish may have been albacore (*Thunnus alalonga*). Albacore is a fairly small tuna that is popular among French and Spanish fishers. The striking row of finlets that Coenen has drawn behind the two dorsal fins is typical of the tuna and mackerel family, the *Scombridae*.

Two tunnies

Here I have illustrated and copied two tunnies, each from a particular book about fish, and each looking rather different from the other.

A lot of tunnies are caught in Constantinople. The tunnies escort the ships there and are not afraid of them. Those tunnies spend the winter in the depths of the sea, and reappear in the summer.

This is a really extremely good illustration of a tunny as I have seen them. These fish can become enormous in size. I've seen one that had to be transported on a big donkey. Aristotle mentions a fish the size of a whale.

The text on the lower right is taken from an unnamed German source, so 'I' does not here refer to Coenen.

The genus *Thunnus* has six tuna species. They are all fast-swimming fish with a torpedo-like body. Most tuna make enormous journeys over the oceans. The bluefin tuna (*T. thynnus*) of the Atlantic is the best known because of its size (it can attain a length of 3 metres), its high price and its exceptional ability to accelerate: a bluefin tuna can reach a speed of 80 kilometres per hour in ten seconds. It can draw in its fins, which fit into grooves, thus increasing its aerodynamic potential.

Tuna fishing did not really get under way until the last decades of the twentieth century, partly because of the high prices in Japan (sushi and sashimi). The most expensive fish in the world was a Southern bluefin tuna: in 2001 the sum of US$ 173,000 was paid for a fish weighing 444 pounds (US$ 391 per pound). In Europe most tuna are caught by fishers in the Mediterranean. Since 1990 tuna fish have also been caught alive and fattened in large cages floating on the sea (sea ranching), before being shipped to Japan.

In the sea there are all kinds of sharks, here and elsewhere

Fish on upper left:

This is among us an *asselhaai*; they have very sharp skins that are put around the hilts of swords.

Fish on lower left:

Among us here in Holland this is the *spiegelhaai*.

Lower left: These are the eggs of these sharks.

With regard to this sort Aristotle writes mainly about the eggs. This fish has a somewhat reddish colour and is dotted with black marks, with a very rough skin that feels like a rasp when you rub it in the wrong direction, from the tail towards the head. The egg of this shark has a sort of shell, is hard and about as translucent as a horn, but with other colours too. Inside is a sort of liquid, just like in an egg. The shape is like that of a pillow with long coils hanging from the end like laces. This fish has unattractive, tough meat and a disgusting smell. Some rays also have eggs like these with coils.

Fish on upper right:

According to the Dutch fishermen, this is the *speerhaai* that the doggers catch in deep water. They are not caught by the coastal fishers.

Two fish on lower right:

These two are the common sharks that are caught in Holland by the fishers; they throw them away. In Zeeland some sharks are called *hinnekens* and they are eaten too.

These common sharks are well known among the fishers in Holland. In the autumn, when the *bolk* comes to our shores, these sharks come as well. They follow the *bolk* and bite it half off from the hooks. Our fishermen also catch them in the summer in the nets. These sharks have many young inside their body. I who write this once found 24 young inside a shark that I cut open to dry it for decoration. The fishers say that the young creep out of the shark's body and go back inside again. Our fishers throw them away: it is not a good fish to eat, but the poor eat them dried or smoked.

Coenen was to lose his dried shark to Spanish freebooters in 1573 (see Introduction). The different sharks on this page are taken from different pages of Pierre Belon's *De aquatilibus, libri duo*, published in Paris in 1553. A French translation of the work, *La nature et diversité des poissons*, appeared in the same city two years later.

The *bolk* is the bib or pout(ing) (*Trisopterus luscus*), a small fish of the cod family with light-coloured bands around its body which can easily be seen at night. A diminutive form, the poor-cod (*P. minutus*), was first recognized as a species in 1965.

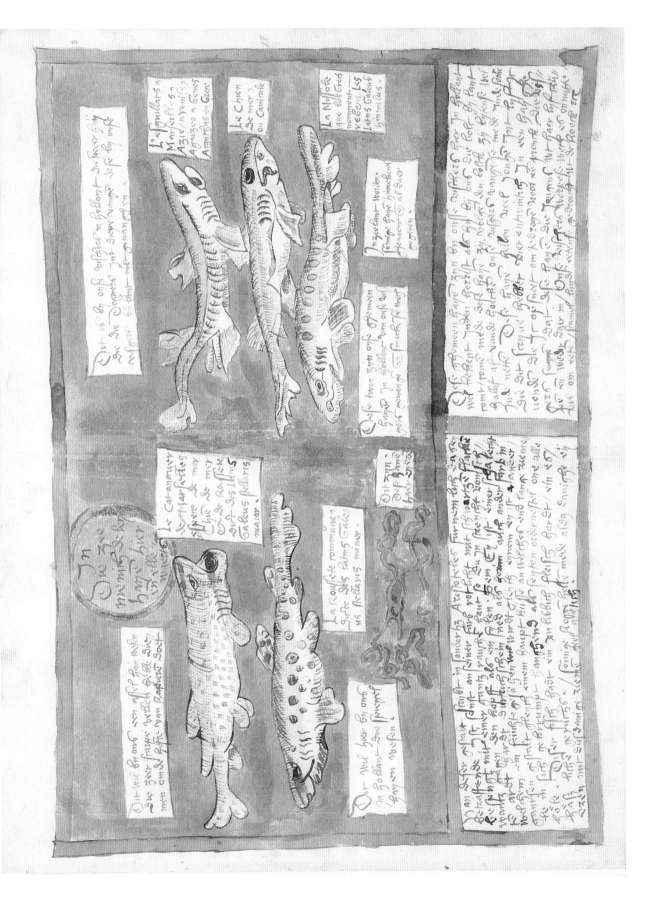

Speerhaai

Upper left: This type of *spitshond* or *doornhond* has been accurately illustrated in Venice.

Lower left: This is a large *speerhaai*, as they are called by fishers in Holland.

Lower right: Galeus centrina.

Not many of these *speerhaaien* were caught by fishers here on the coast of Holland, but there where the doggers fish in the deep for *aberdaan* to salt, they also catch these *speerhaaien*. They cut off the spears and give them to good friends. The rich have the spears mounted in silver and use them as toothpicks. The fishers throw the fish themselves away, but some poor fishers dry them and eat them just like other dried fish.

The following is what the German writes about the big shark illustrated here: Although the meat of this fish used to be praised, the time has come to contradict that. It is a chewy sort of food, difficult to digest, with an unpleasant smell and taste, and is only eaten by the poor when other fish are too expensive.

Coenen here depicts the smaller sharks or dogfish (*Scyliorhinidae*) of the North Sea. The topmost one, labelled Acanthus, is the spurdog or dogfish (*Squalus acanthias*); to the lower left is the small spotted catshark and to the lower right is the tope (*Galeorhinus galeus*).

Dogfish were for a long time considered an unwanted by-catch and were of little commercial importance. By the end of the twentieth century, 30 per cent of the fish sold in fish and chips shops in London was supposedly dogfish. Sharks grow very slowly and do not reproduce until the age of fourteen or more. It therefore takes a very long time for a reduced shark population to recover.

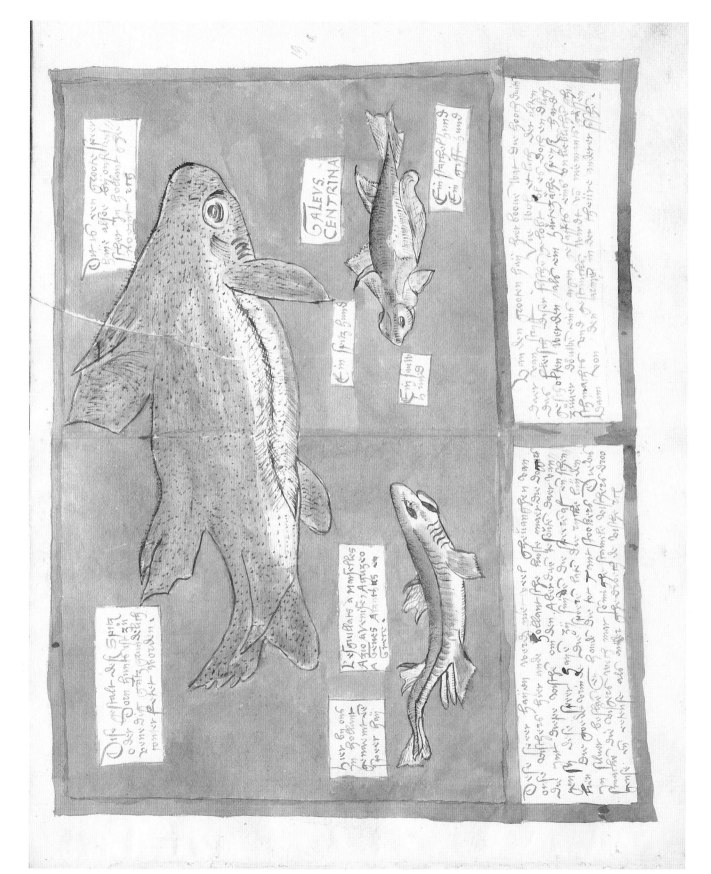

A smooth hound (*toenhaai*), not a tunny

Left-hand figure: This seems to be related to the *toenhaai*. Such large ones do not occur among us. Some people would like to call this a *westerling*, but I do not agree because I once had a *westerling* weighing 300 pounds.

Right-hand figure: This *toenhaai* weighed more than 300 pounds. This *toenhaai* was 11 or 12 feet long.

The *toenhaai* is a big fish and is not suitable for eating by us. It is known to the fishers of Scheveningen, but is not often eaten by them. This fish does not bring in much money. It somewhat resembles the porpoise and has a dullish skin. It is a white, dry fish without oil, which smells terribly. An old saying of ours for when someone smells is: 'You smell like a *toenhaai*'. I who write this once bought a *toenhaai*, salted it and sent it with salted cod in a barrel to Liège. I was supposed to receive nuts in return, but they haven't arrived yet. This fish isn't worth the salt. It is a dry, dull fish. Some poor folk dry it, smoke it and eat it too.

A *toenhaai* was once auctioned on the fish market in Scheveningen, and the clerk of the auction Jacob Symons thanked in advance whoever bought it for removing it from the beach. But no one wanted to give any money for it and the man who had caught it, Willem Gijsgis, had to throw it back into the sea. I cut off the tail and fins to nail to the outside wall of my house. The tail was 11 or 12 feet long.

They say in our village that a man from Egmond once sailed to England – with an east wind, as is usual – with other fishers and took a *toenhaai* to England with him. He sold the *toenhaai* there as a sturgeon, and when this man returned to England later he was hanged because he had pretended that it was a sturgeon. If he had simply sold the fish as *toenhaai*, he wouldn't have been hanged.

The hammerhead on the left is one of the most predatory sharks in the ocean. The European hammerhead (*Sphygna zygnea*) can reach a length of 5 metres and weigh 400 kilograms. The hammerhead is one of the few types of shark that are known to attack humans. Shark populations are very reduced today. Many of them are caught as by-catch in commercial fisheries and there is also a lively market for shark-fin soup in Asia, for which only the dorsal fin is used; the rest of the body is thrown back in the water. The shark on the right may be the smooth hound (*Mustelus mustelus*), a smaller shark of up to 1.5 metres that lives in shallow waters.

The sturgeon was a popular fish in Coenen's days. The sturgeon (*Acipenseridae*), like the salmon, is an anadromous fish that swims up rivers from the sea to spawn. Young sturgeons migrate to the sea when they are three years old. They can live to an age of almost 50 years. The sturgeon is now very rare in western Europe. Caviar, the pickled roe of the sturgeon, comes mainly from Iran and other countries around the Caspian Sea.

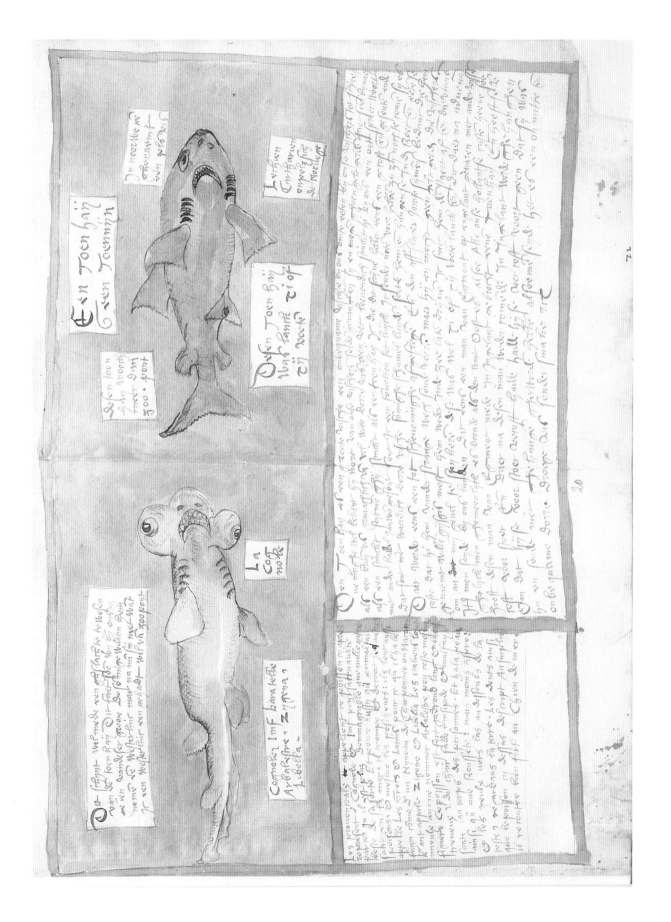

On three unusual fish

Left: Another picture of a *balena*. This one was 14 paces long and his skin was blue, without scales. This remarkable whale was found alive in the Adriatic Sea in 1555.

Upper right: 60 feet long, his skin was without scales and bluish.

Lower right: This one was 68 feet long.

In 1531 a large fish was washed up from the sea in Holland.

In 1551 a large fish was caught in the English sea.

Few people are aware that many whales occur in the Mediterranean, including large ones such as the sperm whale and the fin whale (*Balaenoptera physalus*). To protect the whales, in 1999 the Ligurian Sea, which extends between Corsica, France and Spain, was declared a whale reserve.

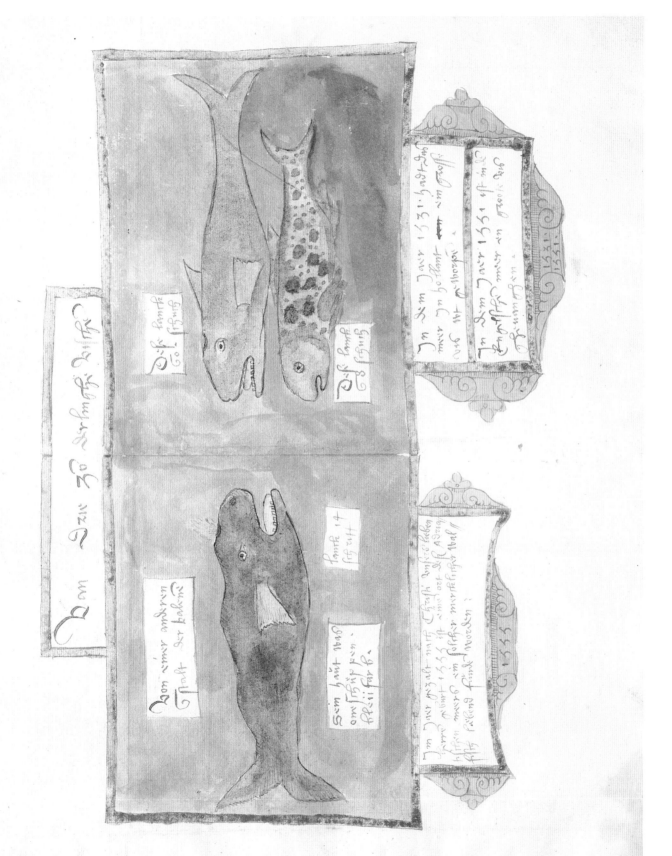

Whale (*Cetus*)

Cetus is the Latin for whale, and all big fish are usually called whales. *Balena* or *belua* are also used.

This instrument is called a harpoon. Fishers aim it at the big fish that come near their ship as described below.

Cetus, a whale, is the largest of all fish. He has a big, wide mouth. He spouts water into the air like clouds, so that he often sinks ships, and he grows so large that no man can catch him. But if the fishers know where the whale is hiding out, they come together with many ships. Then they have flutes on which they play tunefully and they give shrill blasts on the trumpets and with that sound they lure the whale. He comes close to the ships to hear that music and lies on the surface with his back above the water. Then they have a curved instrument with iron teeth like a saw that they throw vigorously into the back, after which they slip away as stealthily and quietly as they can. Not long afterwards he feels the wound and sinks to the seabed, where he wants to rub his back against the bed, but in doing so he drives the iron even deeper into the wound so that it penetrates the layer of fat, touches the flesh, and finally reaches the innermost part of his body. The iron enters the wound with the salt water and kills the whale. When he is dead, he floats up to the surface of the sea again and the fishers return and tie him tightly with large canvases and ropes and bring him joyfully to land. The whale eats nothing but small fish. He attracts them by a sweet vapour that he exhales from his mouth. The fish are attracted by the sweet vapour in his mouth that he has open and he swallows them all. Thus the *Palace of Animals*.

The three big fish that stranded in Westerheij in 1577 had plaice in their mouth. I, Adriaen Coenen, who write this have seen it.

Palace of Animals (*Der dieren palleys*), printed in Brussels in 1520, is a Dutch compilation from the fifteenth-century *Hortus sanitatis*, a work in six books covering the whole of the natural world and including almost 400 woodcuts of animals.

The scientific name for the order of whales and dolphins is *Cetacea*. Before whales were hunted commercially, they were hunted as Coenen describes. Rusty darts were fired or thrown into the whale and the whalers then had to wait for the animal to die of blood poisoning and to rise to the surface. From early times the Inuit of Greenland and the native Americans used a harpoon to which a line with floats was attached.

The Norwegian harpoon illustrated by Coenen is still in use among the Arctic Inuit. Large-scale commercial whaling made a serious advance when the explosive harpoon was invented in Norway in the 1860s. Japanese and Norwegian commercial whalers still use this equipment, which has hardly changed in the last 150 years.

About the *Physeter* and his great cruelty

The *physeter*, which is classified as a whale and is 200 cubits long, has a very cruel nature and temperament, because usually he rises out of the water to wreck ships. He raises himself to above the spirit and blows out through the pipes on top of his head the water that he has taken in, so that with a huge tremendous flood of water he often causes the biggest and strongest ships to go under or at least puts the crew at risk of drowning. He has a black and thick skin all over his body, long fins like wide feet, and a forked tail, which is 15 or 20 feet wide and with which he holds the ships very tightly. Nevertheless the seamen have a very effective remedy against malice, and that is a trumpet. He cannot stand its loud and harsh sound at all. As a second remedy they also throw tremendously large barrels into the sea with which they try to stop the beast from approaching because he starts to play with these barrels. They also fire large pieces of artillery to frighten the beast with the din rather than to wound it, because iron or stone cannonballs lose their power in the water and also have little capacity to harm such a large body because of the animal's layer of fat.

I tell you too that near the coasts of Norway various monsters are very often spotted – sometimes familiar ones, sometimes new and unknown ones – that mainly come from the unfathomable depths of the sea where many kinds of fish live that are rarely or never seen by humans.

Pistris is a large beast in the sea that has been found several times in the ocean sea. This beast sometimes stands up in the sea like a large column and throws itself on to the sails of the ships. It blows a lot of water into the ships, so that the men on board find themselves in great difficulty.

Tinnus is a sea monster with a tail two cubits wide. It bears its young in the sea and goes on land to eat. It follows ships out of curiosity to watch them sailing and is like the *tigris* which I have described elsewhere.

Physeter is *Physeter macrocephalus*, the sperm whale. *Physeter* means 'blower'. *Macrocephalus* (literally 'long-headed') refers to its large head, which measures more than 30 per cent of the total body length. The sperm whale was often identified as the living Leviathan (the large sea monster mentioned in Job 40 and 41). Behaviour research in the twentieth century has revealed that, contrary to Coenen's statement that it is 'a cruel animal', the sperm whale is not particularly aggressive.

A young *hil* that was beached in Scheveningen on 28 June 1581

The Prince of Orange saw this fish in Scheveningen when he came there. This fish had a big salmon in its throat when it was cut open. The fishers said it was a young *hil* that had choked on the salmon.

This fish was washed up dead on the shore near Scheveningen in the year 1581. My brother Jan Coenen had it taken to the village with a float and ropes (because he is shoreman to the steward Jenits), because the fish was first washed up north of the village. Some measured him and arrived at a length of 15 feet, others 16 feet. The news that a fish had been washed up soon reached The Hague, so that a lot of people came to Scheveningen to see this fish, including the Prince of Orange. We talked a lot about fish and about my other big fish book that I had previously given to him, and I asked him if he would take on my son to be educated; I wanted to thank him. There was another gentleman there who said: 'Give your son to my lord.' I said: 'Sir, I shall have to think it over.' The prince said: 'Come and see me tomorrow in The Hague, and if you have something unusual of a fishy sort bring it with you.' The prince's wife gave my son a gold coin. The next day I went to The Hague and took the prince two dried sepias and handed them over personally. His wife said: 'Father will reward you.' And since the bad news that Breda had fallen had just been announced, the court was in a depressed state. The prince had a pound sent to me and the bringer of the reward said: 'My lord is now a poor gentleman. Another time he will be able to give you more.'

Breda fell to the Spanish on 27 June 1581. Coenen first gave a fish book (now presumably lost) to William of Orange in 1574. His son, Coenraet van Schilperoort (1577–1636), who was a young boy at the time of this incident (see inset), later became a landscape and portrait painter in Leiden.

Although the proportions are not accurate, the length, black colouring, white belly and above all the shape of the fins indicate a long-finned pilot whale (*Globicephala melaena*). Some types of whale – the pilot whale and sometimes the sperm whale – occasionally strand on beaches in large numbers. Mass strandings of whales still form a phenomenon that is not entirely understood. It has been suggested that their acoustic mechanisms for keeping on course do not function in shallow water; that they can detect magnetic fields; or that they are conducting a sick whale to his last resting-place.

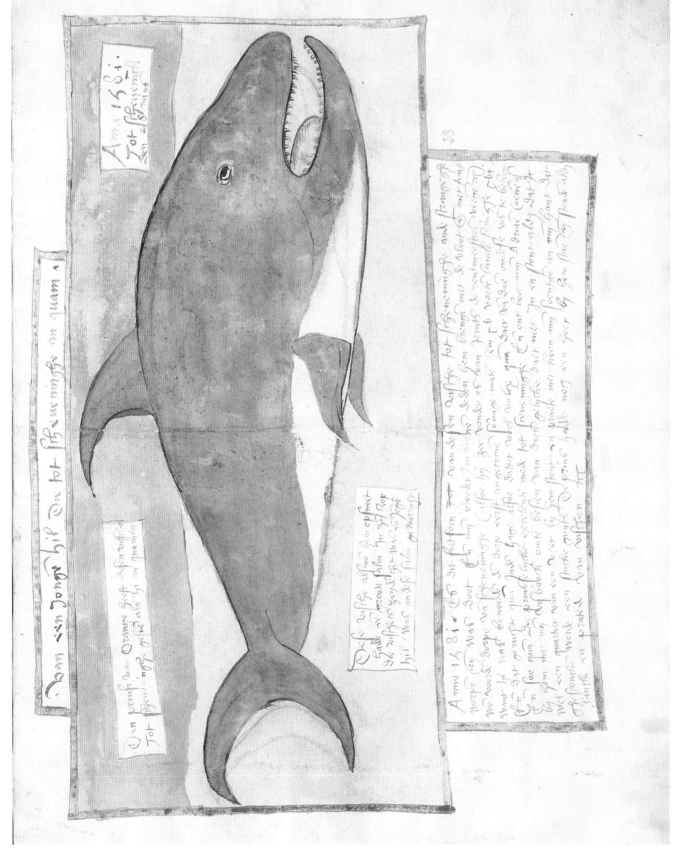

47

About a wondrous fish that was found in North England in 1532

It was 90 feet long. In the harvest month of the year 1532, a very large and very rare monster was washed up on the shore of Tynemouth. It was partly torn, but there was still enough left to fill a hundred carts. According to the source on which this information is based, there was an intolerable stench on the 26th day of the harvest month, when the creature was still there. The beast had 30 ribs in its side, with a length of 21 feet, three stomachs the size of very deep cellars, thirty throats, of which 5 were very big, and 2 fins, each 15 feet long. Reports on its tongue vary, but most say it was 7 ells long. The teeth were like the horns of an animal and its eyes were small in proportion to the body. They said that its sheath was wondrously big, a male. When they were cutting the beast open someone almost drowned because he fell into its belly; he would have come to a bad end if he hadn't been able to grab a rib with his hand and hold on to that. After I had written this, I saw an illustration of this fish, and it looked exactly like the three fish that were beached near Westerheij in 1577.

Coenen's source here is presumably an English pamphlet about this 'wondrous fish'.

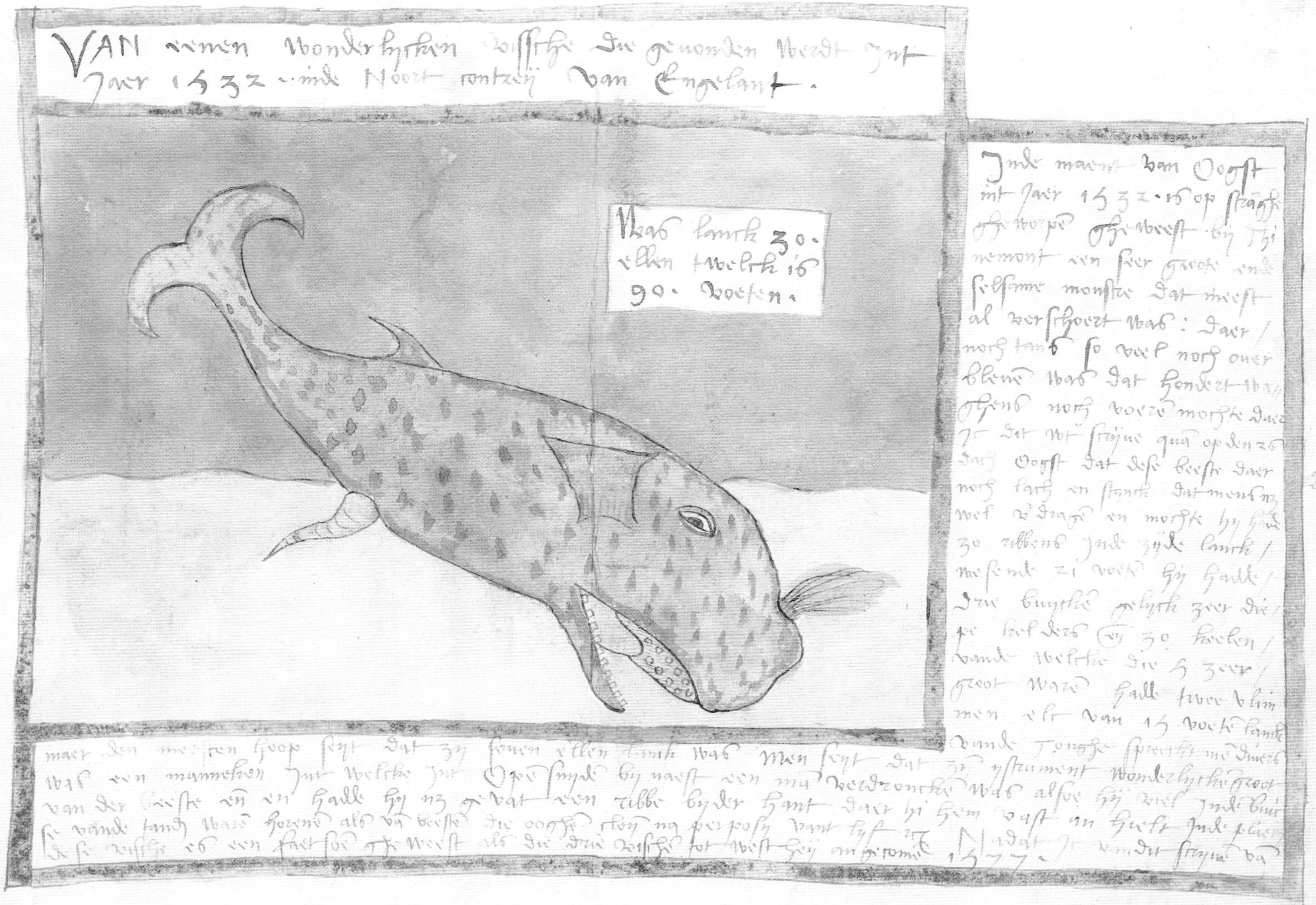
VAN eenen wonderlycken visshe die gevonden werdt int Jaer 1532 inde Noort contrey van Engelant.
Was lanck 30 ellen twelck is 90 voeten.

About a big fish that swallowed a small boat with two men on board

I was told, and assured that it was true, that a big ship was once anchored off Norway. Two of the crew went out sailing in a small boat or sloop for pleasure because it was fine weather. While they were sailing, a big fish came along that swallowed the boat, men and all. But because the big fish couldn't digest the boat and was troubled by it, he was washed up and floated back and forth just off the coast. The people who lived there came and cut it open and chopped the fish in pieces. Once it had been opened, they found a small boat in the fish with two men: one was dead, the other was still alive. The one who was still alive had been near the front close to the fish's mouth. His hair had been singed off his head by the heat; the dead man had been buried deeper in the body.

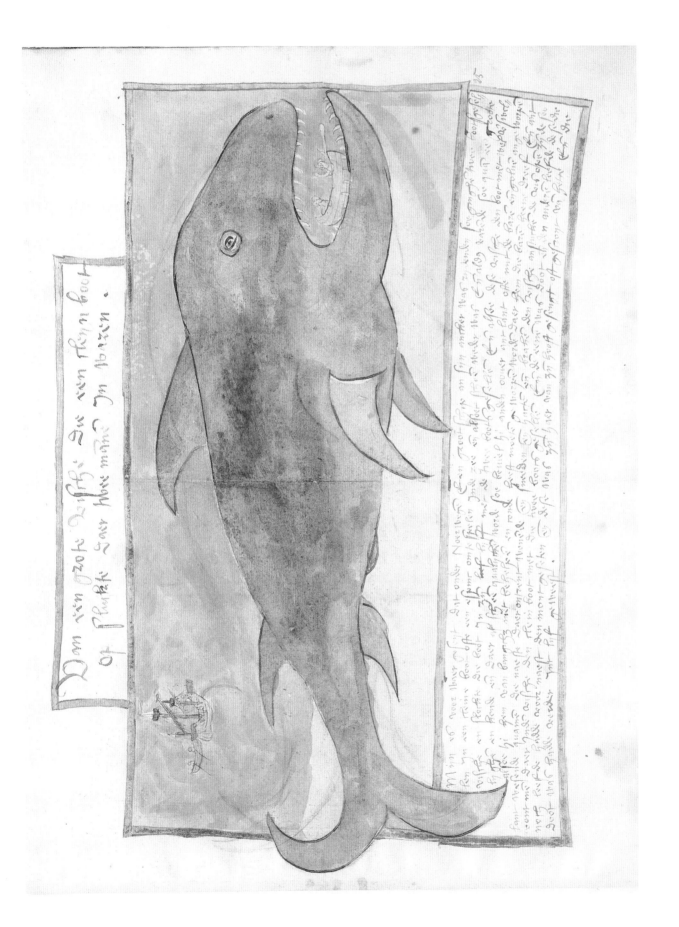

51

On the swordfish, unicorn and sawfish as Olaus describes them

Left-hand fish: This has a sword on the back.

Upper right-hand fish: This has a saw on the back.

Lower right-hand fish: This has a large sharp horn on its head.

These fish cause great damage to the ships off Norway. The fact that these savage creatures are found in the North Sea is the reason why I include them here among the other rare fish, because the swordfish looks a bit like a whale. Its head is rough and hairy like the barn owl, its mouth is very deep like a deep pool. Those who look at it are terrified and driven away by it. This fish has terrible eyes, a sharp jaw and a sword on its back. It causes great damage to the ships that sail the coasts of Norway because it pierces them like a real robber to make them sink.

The unicorn is a sea monster with a very long horn on its forehead with which it pierces the ships it comes across, so that it ruins many ships and causes very many people to drown. But God in his benevolence has given seamen a remedy against the savagery of these beasts: since they swim very sluggishly, the seamen who spot them in the distance can easily avoid them and sail around them.

The sawfish is also a sea monster, with a large body, and a sharp comb on top of its head with teeth like a sword. He saws through ships from below by swimming back and forth beneath them, to make the ships sink so that he can indulge in the meat of drowned men. There is another sort of sawfish that raises its saw against the seamen. When they have followed the ships four or five times they disappear again, exhausted, to the depths of the sea. When a fisher is wounded by the sword on the back of this orca, he loses consciousness and if you touch him by the hand it immediately loses all feeling. This is all written in Olaus.

The only animal that can be taken to be a unicorn is the narwhal (*Monodon monoceros*), an Arctic whale that can grow to a length of 5 metres. The narwhal does not have any teeth, but the male has a spiral tusk protruding from the left jaw that can be as long as 3 metres. A tusk is rare among females. Its function is unclear. It may be used to turn over the seabed, to break the ice, or to fight for a mate. Narwhals are particularly found in the west Atlantic Ocean. At least 20,000 of them come from the high North and meet in Lancaster Sound and off West Greenland every summer.

Coenen may well have seen one of the narwhal tusks, often identified as the horns of unicorns, that were common in collections of curiosities in the sixteenth century.

The swordfish are also classified as whales because they can be 10 ells big

Left-hand fish: Gladius is a fish that owes its name to the shape of its jaw. It grows with a sharp mouth like a sword and uses it to pierce the ships to wreck them.

On Friday after St Martin's Day in 1576 in the winter, a fisher in Scheveningen called Hendrik Jans alias Jan Heinszoon caught a swordfish among all sorts of other fish. It was about 10 feet long and half a barrel wide, it was said. He ate some of it, gave some pieces of fish to other people, and pickled the rest to eat it later. He nailed the head with the protruding sword to his house. I came to Scheveningen at this time, when I lived in Leiden but had left because of the plundering soldiers from Haarlem, that had not yet sided with the prince. Then I bought this fish's head with sword for the price of his drinking his fill of English beer for one day.

At the time of writing this sword is still with Abel the goldsmith who lives in Delft near the Nieuwe Kerk. I gave it to him in exchange for other things. The sword was 1 ell 4 thumbs long and the width of a cutlass. This was the first swordfish I saw. There was also a fisher in Rotterdam who had caught one, and I saw that swordfish there. It was as long and wide as the previous one.

What the Germans write about swordfish: This is a very beautiful, good-natured, large and noble fish, that owes its name to its appearance, for its upper jaw grows in length in the shape of a sharp sword. The fish can achieve a very great length of more than 10 ells. Its sword or beak consists of a very hard substance, like hard bone, which does not lose its sharpness on stone. Occasionally it grows to the size of a whale and then its sword looks like a large oar.

In 1583 a dead swordfish was on show for money here in Holland in Amsterdam, Delft and a few other cities. It brought the people showing it a lot of money.

Martinmas or St Martin's Day falls on 11 November. The prince is William of Orange, leader of the Dutch Revolt against Habsburg rule.

The swordfish (*Xiphias gladius*) roams the oceans alone or in small groups. The largest ever found was more than 5 metres long. It has been heavily overfished, but international regulation to save this beautiful fish from further depletion has proved difficult.

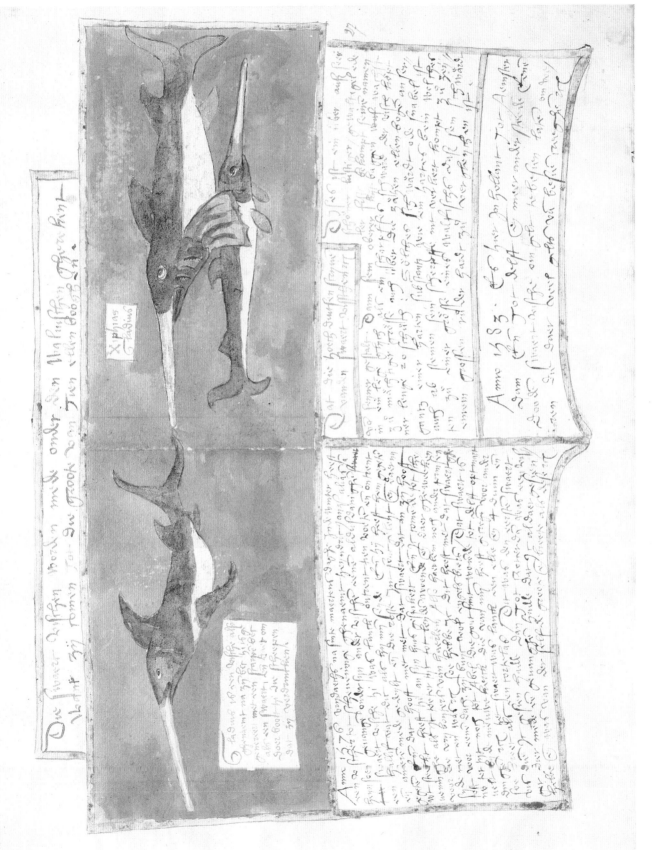

About the sproeivis, zeebok and zeesprinkhaan

The largest fish in the Indian sea is said to be the sprinkler fish (*sproeivis*). In these far seas there are fish that rise out of the water like a large column and expel vast quantities of water like a cloudburst over the sails and masts of a ship. The Germans call all big fish whales, or balena or porpoise. They copy the old ichthyologists, but I attach most credence to the people who live close to the sea and experience it every day.

The sea goat (*zeebok*) behaves at sea like other predators. He lurks in the shadow of a big ship and waits until someone goes into the water to bathe, or he waits somewhere else, raises his head just above the water, and when a fisher comes swimming by he swims furtively after him and seizes the chance to toss him or to catch him in some other way.

Locusta marina is the locust of the sea and looks just like the land locust. According to Pliny he is 4 cubits long and grows lean in the winter, when he hides himself for five months in underwater caves. He reappears when it is nice and warm in May, and then he grows fat again. He also grows big and full-grown in the autumn and at full moon. They live mainly in water where there are a lot of stones. The *polippus* fish avoids this sea locust so much that it dies of fright when it sees it.

Pliny the Elder, a Roman polymath who died during the eruption of Vesuvius in AD 79, wrote the highly influential *Historia naturalis* (*Natural History*). Coenen knew it via Johannes Heyden's German version, which was published in Frankfurt in 1565.

The whale that jumps most frequently clear out of the water (breaching) is the humpback whale (*Megaptera novaeangliae*), although sperm whales and occasionally other baleen whales can also be seen breaching. Various descriptions indicate that although most humpbacks migrate annually to low latitudes, there are resident humpbacks in the northern Indian Ocean.

The sea locust is reminiscent of the mud-skippers (*Periopthalminae*) of Africa and Asia. Mudskippers have a high forehead and bulging eyes. They can grow to a length of 25 centimetres and are mainly found in brackish water in mangroves and pools. They dig themselves in during the dry season and reappear in the rainy season.

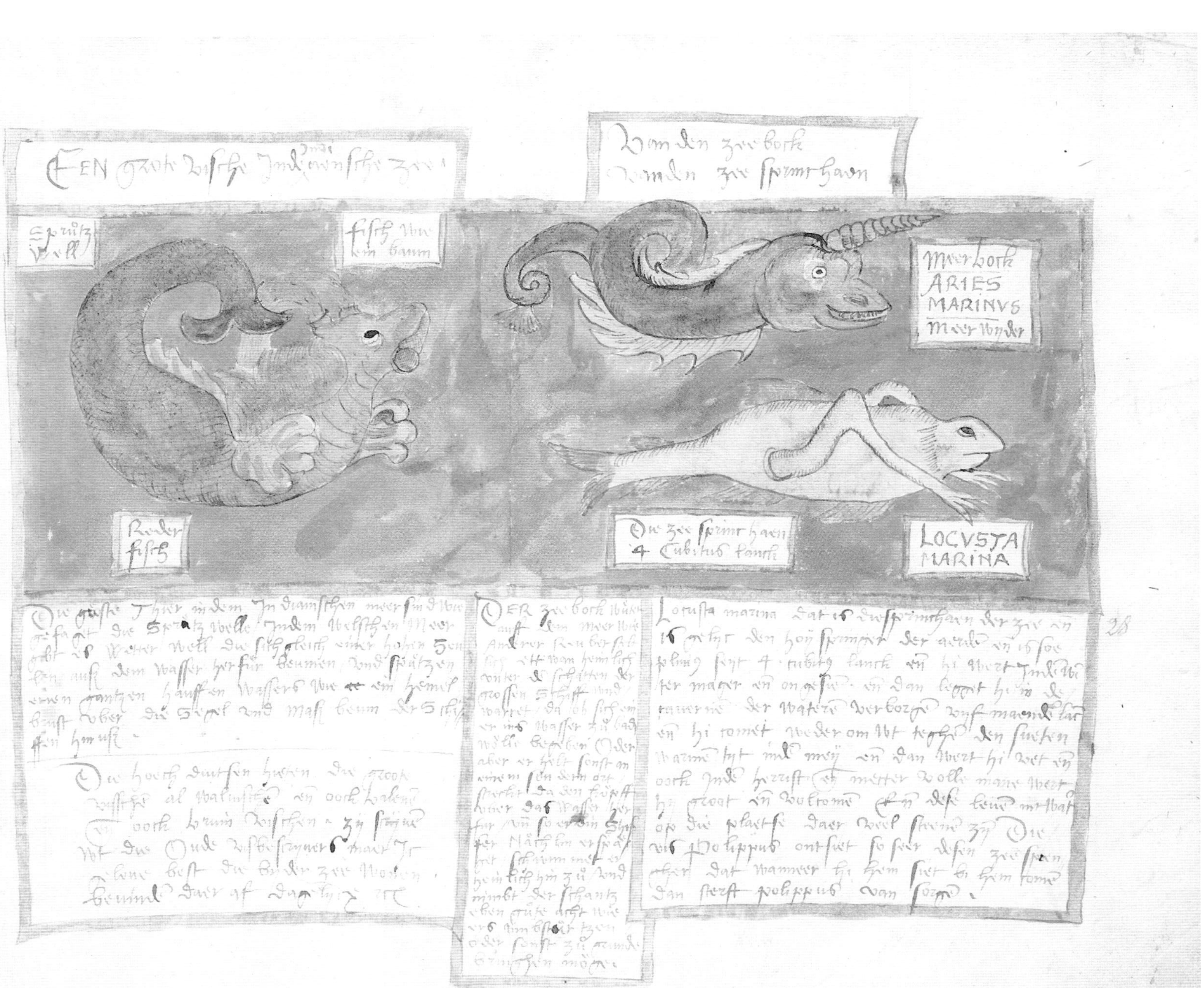

MARIMOTP
ARIES MARINVS
Mant Worder

LOCVSTA
MARINA

En zee Spine haen
4 Cubitus tonne

Wanden zee bote
wanden zee Vram haen

CEN Grate Duste Duckwir fisse Zwar

fisse dem
xm haem

Puder
fiß

Spmiz
fiß

Platanistae in the River Ganges

Upper left: Some of them are 60 ells long.

Upper right: Common balena or whale.

Below left-hand fish: These fish are so strong that they can drag an elephant into the water. In the River Ganges in India is a fish that is called *Platanista*. It reaches a size of about 15 ells. Statius Sebosius reports as a mighty wonder that various rare creatures live in the same river that have two gills. They are about 60 ells long, are sky blue in colour, and it is said that the shape of their body is a half-dragon. These fish are so enormously strong that they seize elephants who come to drink by the trunk and drag them beneath the water. 1584.

Statius and Sebosius are two of the Latin writers on whom Pliny the Elder drew for his *Natural History.* Coenen apparently conflates them.

The river dolphin that is found in the Ganges and the Indus is the susu (*Platanista gangetica*). River dolphins are the only species with a flattened jaw like the one depicted by Coenen on the left. The susu is blind (sight is not particularly useful in the muddy Ganges) and swims on its side along the river bed with its head slightly raised. The fish depicted on the right resembles the finless porpoise (*Neophocaena phocaenoides*), a member of the porpoise family that is found all over Asia in estuaries and swims far up the rivers. The finless porpoise is grey, but once dead it soon turns black. Both dolphins are relatively small (2 to 2.5 metres).

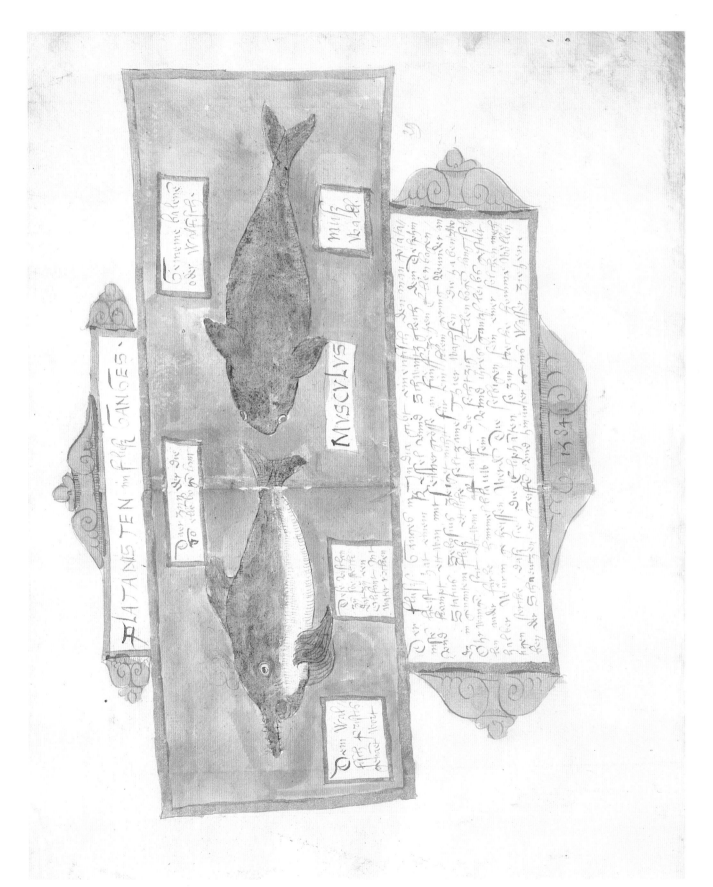

59

On the catching of fish and how it can provide knowledge about the future

How a fish announced a future victory to the Emperor Augustus. Fish also give indications of future events, as when Emperor Augustus was walking along the shore during the Sicilian war and a big fish jumped out of the water and landed right in front of his feet. It has been interpreted and explained as the announcement of prosperity and something good. Sextus Pompeius had to expect the opposite: he was to be defeated and to come off as the loser. That is also what subsequently happened, since the emperor demonstrated such superiority in the war at sea that all had to surrender to him who had been lord and master of the sea and of the great waters until then.

Sextus Pompeius, son of Gnaeus Pompeius Magnus, occupied Sicily after the murder of his father in Egypt in 48 BC. He was defeated at sea twelve years later. The episode of the fish is related in Suetonius' *Life of Augustus*.

Torpedo

Whoever touches this fish will find that his limbs are paralysed and deadened and its poison even runs along the hook. This happens when the creature is alive.

Aristotle writes that a large torpedo was once sighted with 80 young inside it. There are quite a lot of such fish in the River Nile.

This fish lurks on the sea bed and waits for other fish to approach it; those who come too close are paralysed. He catches them and eats them, and that is his way of collecting food, for he is a sluggish swimmer.

Torpedo is the scientific name for the electric ray. Coenen depicts the marbled electric ray (*Torpedo marmora*). The common electric ray (*T. nobiliana*) is brownish-black. Rays wait in the mud for their prey, then wrap themselves around it and stun it with electric shocks. The electric organs on either side of the electric ray's head can generate shocks of 220 volts/8 amps.

Rays are often caught accidentally by fishermen trawling for sole and plaice. As a result, they have become extremely rare in the North Sea. However, the sighting of a marbled electric ray has always been unusual there.

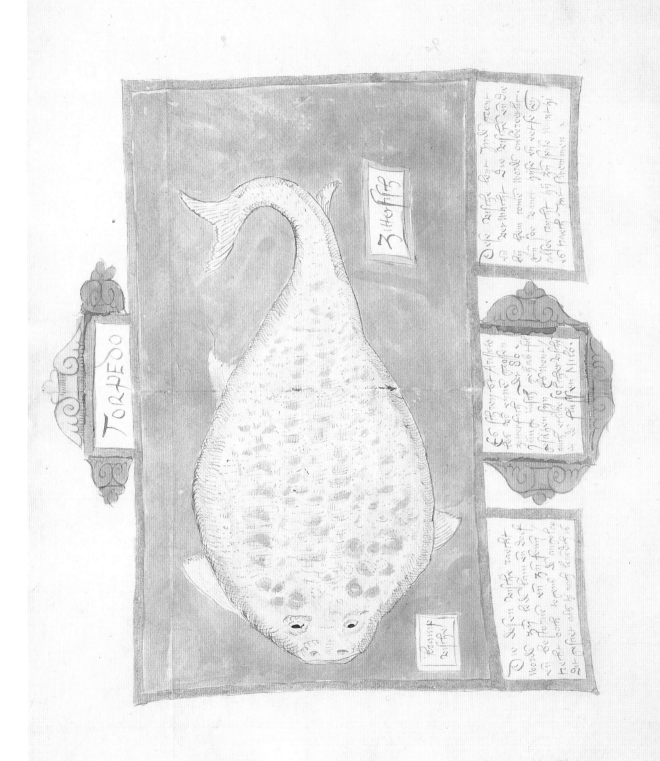

63

About *zeevarkens* [sea swine]

Left: As illustrated in Olaus.

Right: As illustrated in the *Palace of Animals*.

I have copied this from Olaus, Bishop of Uppsala. We have already written about a wondrous fish that was found off the coasts of England, and in particular about the one that was seen there in the year 1532, with a clear description of its whole body. But I shall here write about the wondrous pig that was found later, in the year 1537, in the German sea. It was strange and rare in all of its body parts, for it had the head of a pig and a sort of mane at the back of its head. It had four feet like a dragon, and on each side two eyes and a third on the belly near the navel, but it also had a forked tail like other fish. Thus the description by Olaus.

I have copied this from the *Palace of Animals*. This source does not give any length, width or colour, but represents the creature with scales. It is a short report about a rare fish. I think that more should be written about it. The sea swine looks like the terrestrial pig, because when the sea swine is looking for food, it roots in the soil of the sea bed too. Its head is just like that of a pig, and so are its limbs and ribs. Its body is just like that of a pig, with oily fat. It has several needles or bristles on its back that contain a strong poison. Anyone who is pricked by them will feel a lot of pain, but the creature's gall is the best remedy. The sea swine has a tongue like a terrestrial pig, but it makes a very different noise. I have copied this from an old book called the *Palace of Animals*, which was printed more than 60 years ago. I wrote this on Martinmas 1584 (according to the new almanac).

About the sea angel or *squatina*

This fish looks like our *schoerhaai* or *scheervis*, but otherwise is not much like what I wrote about it in my *Big Fish Book*.

This sea angel reached me from Venice. Its portrait was made by someone there from life. This fish can achieve a considerable size, as big as a person and weighing as much as 160 pounds.

This is an angel shark or monkfish, *Squatina squatina*. Nowadays the angel shark is caught for human consumption in northern Europe. It can attain a weight of 80 kilograms with a length of 2.5 metres. It looks very like a ray, but is classified as a shark because its pectoral fins have not entirely disappeared. Like other sharks, the angel shark is a cartilaginous fish. It has no scales, but the structure of its skin is like a rasp. Most sharks are viviparous; some lay eggs of the same shape as ray eggs.

A strange whale

Valentius Gravius, a citizen of Freiburg, sent this depiction of this whale to Conrad Gessner, the great and famous ichthyologist. 1584.

Why is the penis always so prominent in illustrations of stranded whales? It is an internal organ in living whales and is only extruded during copulation. When a whale dies, however, the muscle that retains the penis no longer functions, so that the penis is extruded. The penis of a sperm whale can be more than 1 metre long and that of the blue whale, the largest animal that ever lived on earth, almost 2 metres.

Prints of beached whales often show figures engaged in measuring the length of the penis. The preserved penis was a regular feature of Renaissance collections of curiosities.

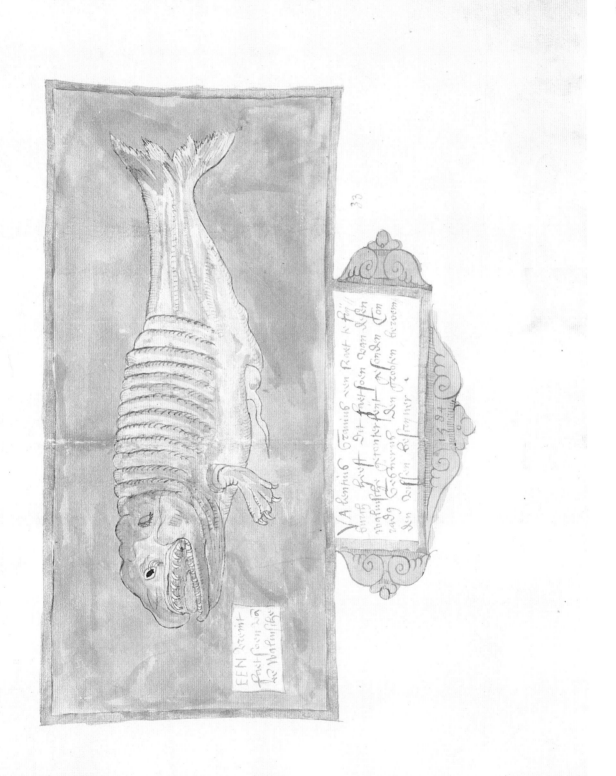

Two orcas, each unusual in appearance

Left: An orca with a smooth skin like a porpoise.

Right: An orca with scales.

Rondelet says that when the orca attacks the balena, he bites it to death as if it were an ox. I have also illustrated how the orcas attack and bite the whales. This creature attacks the whales in their shelters. It also attacks pregnant whales and rips open their bellies. 1584. I found this picture of the orca in the same German source from which I have taken this text.

Guillaume Rondelet (1507–1556), professor of medicine at Montpellier, was the author of *Libri de piscibus marini* (1554) and *Universae aquatilium pars altera* (1555), which were both very often bound in a single volume. A French edition, *L'Histoire entière des poissons*, was published in Lyon in 1558.

The only enemy to be feared by large whales apart from *homo sapiens* is the orca. Underwater observation and acoustic research off the west coast of Canada have made it possible to distinguish two types of orcas: the resident population that lives mainly on salmon and displays a friendly and social behaviour, and the transients that terrorize the other orcas with their aggressive and anti-social behaviour.

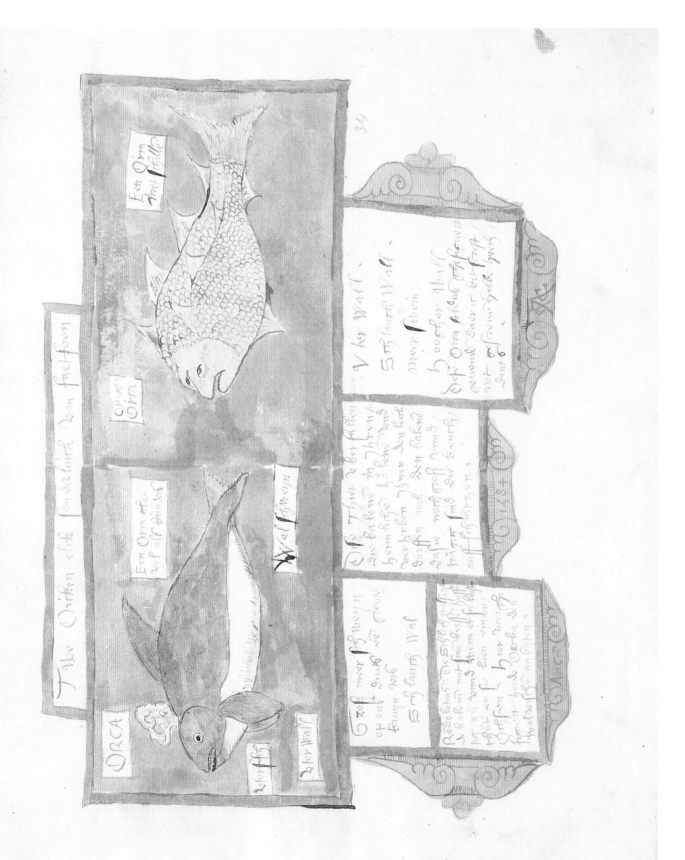

About whale-catching and whale sperm

Left: Whales are caught between cliffs.

Middle: Purified whale sperm is called amber.

Right: This is the sperm that whales ejaculate.

Since whales are very keen on herring and other oily fish, they often run great risks near the sandbanks because at ebb the water recedes and these cruel beasts are left lying on the sand without being able to reach the deeper water close to them. Then they become so enraged that they make a deep well in the sand with their tail and then lie in it as though they were sitting in a nest and couldn't get out again. When the fishers get wind of this, they flock there in large numbers and bring strong ropes and anchors with them to prevent the beasts from escaping and drifting away at flood tide. They use them to bind these creatures and then drag them with great effort on to the dry land. If such an adventure concludes well, they share the booty with one another, and afterwards each one goes home to concern himself with his own affairs until something similar happens again.

Whales propagate in the same way as men and women, but the male ejaculates an over-abundance of sperm, so that the female cannot retain it all and the sperm is spread in the sea water. It is different in appearance and blue or blue-grey-white in colour, and forms a strongly adhesive mass. It is eagerly sought and collected by the fishers (as I have seen at sea, writes Olaus) when it floats on the surface of the water, because they sell it to apothecaries to be purified. When it has been purified it is called amber or ambergris. They use it to make a salve that they regard as the best and most effective remedy against rheumatism and lack of energy. Some amber is white, but grey amber is the best. An imitation amber is also produced, using aloe powder, wood, storax and other medicines, but it is not difficult to recognize. Imitation amber immediately becomes soft like wax, but real amber hardly melts at all. It has a very healing and consoling effect, and is good for falling sickness and a weak heart.

Coenen confuses two whale products. The spermaceti is found in the bulbous head and was popular for its high oil qualities. The other product in a sperm whale is ambergris. Sperm whales produce ambergris in the intestines in reaction to squid bones. Grey ambergris was highly praised as an ointment. It was always a surprise how much ambergris would be found in a dead sperm whale. In 1913 more than £23,000 was paid for a piece of ambergris weighing just over 1,000 pounds.

Storax is a fragrant resinous substance obtained by boiling the wood of certain trees. It is used in the preparation of medicines and perfumes.

On the great love of whales for their young, and the *zwamvis*

O people, how the animals love their young! The whales who have no jaws blow through two tubes, but, nevertheless, this is only found among a very few fish. If the young whales are ill or weak, they are carried by the old, but if they are still very small they carry the young between their teeth. They do the same if a storm is brewing, and after the storm they let the young out again. If the young are unable to follow their parents from lack of water, the parents fill their jaws with water and spout it towards the young like a river, so that they can get off the sandbank they are stuck on. Moreover, the parents still accompany the young for a long time after they have grown up, because they soon grow in size and continue to grow for ten years.

The *zwamvis* is a wondrous fish that curls itself up like a hedgehog. Among all kinds of monstrous fish that are found near Norway there is also a round monster called *zwamvis* in Norwegian. It is the greediest and meanest of all creatures. People say that it is never satisfied, but that it does not have a special stomach. That is why everything it eats is immediately digested and turned into body fat, so that the creature looks like nothing but a curled up lump of fat. It grows very broad and expands, but when it cannot expand any further it spews the fish it has eaten out of its mouth again. Like other fish, it has no neck: its mouth is attached directly to its stomach. This creature is so fat that it draws its skin and flesh over its head when danger threatens, just like the hedgehog, and remains concealed like that. However, it harms itself in the process, for from fear of a hostile creature it does not uncurl again when it is hungry, but eats its own flesh and lives on itself. It prefers to eat a part of itself than to be entirely swallowed up by other beasts. But when it sees that the danger is over, it finds a safe spot.

Whales and dolphins are considered to be social animals. The group behaviour of dolphins shows their level of social development. When they hunt, they organize and coordinate the different tasks. Sick or wounded dolphins are assisted by their fellow dolphins. Care of their young is extensive and is accompanied by complex behaviour.

On all kinds of whales and other kinds of strange fish from Olaus

There are all kinds of whales. Some are hairy and are the size of 4 *gemeten* of land: a *gennet* is 240 foot long and 120 wide. Some are without hair, but the ones that are caught in the Western and Norwegian seas are smaller. Others have a long mouth, 12 to 14 feet long, full of teeth. These kinds of whales have a mouth that is suitable for eating and big eyes that are so wide that 15 or even 20 people could sit in the round part of the eye. They have 250 horns above each eye, six or seven feet long, that are as hard as horns. They contract them when they are in danger, but also for fun, or to protect their eyes from other fish. Afterwards I shall discuss the size of the ribs and bones and their uses, as well as the hides, flesh and train-oil. Thus writes Olaus.

From the various sorts of fish that you see here you can tell that there is a large variety of different fish in the North Sea whose names, use, character and properties have been described neither by philosophers nor by any other author. They include a small fish, about a palm in size, with the head of a hare and sharp fins on its back, that terrifies all other fish with its gaze alone and kills many people. There is also a fish with a horn on its head and a mouth on its belly. It is lean and not tasty to eat. There are also fish like bows, with a big head like a buffalo. They are good to eat and their skins are used to make slippers. Thus writes Olaus.

Olaus writes that churches and houses are made from the ribs of whales, and doors from whaleskin

In the countries where there are many large whales, that is in the Northern countries, the people often use the ribs of whales and other large monsters to make houses and chapels and for household utensils. For if these very big fish are driven on to dry land by the force of other creatures that are their enemies, or are caught and dragged on to land by human skill, and then they lie rotten and used up on the sand, or all the meat and train-oil has been used by people, then it is clear that the big bones will not simply be left lying there unused. They can be used to make whole houses, walls, doors, window-frames, roofs, benches and tables. These ribs are 20 or 30 or more feet long. And then there are the pieces of the spinal column and the large split bones of the head, which through the skill of the craftsmen are fitted into one another with files and saws so neatly that a carpenter couldn't do a better job with iron nails. Olaus describes this in his 21st book on the countries of the North.

When there is no more flesh left on the bones and the entrails have been removed, there is not much of these large fish left except the bones, which lie there like big ships that lie upside-down with the hull upwards. After a while they are cleaned by the rain and the air, and then groups of people toil to erect them as houses. Window-frames are made from them in the tops of the roofs or in the side, and they are divided up into many comfortable homes. But the doors are made from the skin of these creatures, which has been removed long before and hardened in the biting wind. Separate stalls are made for pigs and other animals in these houses, just as people do in other kinds of houses. There is always some space left under the roof for the cockerels, which are there instead of clocks to wake people up in the night to go and work, because it is night there the whole winter long. People who sleep beneath these whale ribs often dream that they are in great danger at sea and are at risk of drowning in a storm. This is what Olaus writes.

The illustration shows bones and vertebrae. The doors of the houses may have been made of the skins of seals or walruses, but not of whaleskin, which is a very thin covering over a thick layer of blubber.

About Jonah who had been swallowed

O how wonderfully does God almighty work through big fish. Jonah is swallowed by a big fish and then spewed out again on land, as you can read in the Bible where it is written.

The reference is to the four chapters of the Old Testament book of Jonah.

How the angel warned Tobias so that the fish would not swallow him

One can believe from this that many fish are medicinal. Tobias set out with his dog. The first evening he stayed beside the River Tigris, where he chose to wash his feet. And behold, a big fish appeared, to swallow him up. Tobias shouted: 'Lord, he's heading my way.' And the angel said to him: 'Seize him and drag him towards you.' When he had done so, he dragged it on dry land and the fish began to wriggle at his feet. Then the angel said to him: 'Remove the entrails of this fish and keep its heart, gall and liver, for they are useful as medicines.' When he had done so, he prepared the flesh of the fish, and took some with him on his journey. When they came to Rages, the city of the Medes, Tobias asked the angel: 'Brother Azariah, I pray that you tell me what powers these parts of the fish have that I had to preserve.' And the angel answered and said to him: 'If you place a piece of the heart on the coals, its smoke will drive away all sorts of devils, so that they do not appear any more. And the gall is useful as a salve for eyes which have a fleck on them, after which they will be healthy again.'

The story of Tobias' journey to Rages (or Media, according to some ancient authorities) is told in Chapter Six of the apocryphal book of Tobit.

Silurus

This is a representation of our catfish.

This awesome creature could be called *walvis* in German. It was unknown to scholars for a long time because it was only caught in certain rivers in Germany. It is a very ugly, large and harmful fish. It grows to 7 or 8 ells long. As a young fish it is blackish with white spots; once it is old and large the spots grow whitish. It has terribly wide jaws and a very big head, no teeth but just jaws. It has no scales but a smooth, slippery skin.

The catfish (*Silurus glanis*) is a freshwater fish that is widely farmed today for consumption. It has six sensors attached to its strikingly large jaw: two 'antennae' on its head, two beneath the corners of the mouth, and two on the lower jaw. In the Netherlands catfish are occasionally caught as by-catch in rivers, large lakes and in the IJsselmeer. A large catfish can weigh 40 kilograms and have a length of 1.8 metres. Catfish in Britain are usually smaller, but much larger ones are found in eastern Europe. The largest catfish ever recorded was in a commercial fishery in the River Dnepr in Russia; it weighed more than 325 kilograms and was 5 metres long.

On terrible sea monsters off the coasts of Norway, as Olaus describes them in his 21st book

This fish has many horns, up to 250, around its eyes. You can't represent these fish as strangely as Olaus describes them. Olaus writes very wonderful things about these fish, but they are not credible.

Dolphin and balena

The fastest and speediest animal of all is the dolphin, not only among all wonders and fish of the sea, but also faster than a bird, yes, even faster than an arrow. If his prey is not swimming too far below him and is straight ahead, no fish can escape him. 1584.

The balenas and dolphins have no gills: they breathe through tubes that lead to their lungs. But the balena's tubes run from the forehead, the dolphin's from the back.

There is a large variation in speed between the different whale and dolphin species. Right whales and bowhead whales swim very slowly, which is why they could be hunted by boats that had no engines. Blue and fin whales are much faster, so they could not be hunted until the advent of the steam-driven boat in the late nineteenth century. Dolphins can generally swim faster than large whales. The fastest member of the whale family on record was a great orca, which reached a speed of 55 km/h.

On the monster *delphinus* in the *Book of the Nature of Things* as described in chapter 27 of the *Palace of Animals*

Upper left: Our porpoises also breastfeed their young.

Lower left: Our porpoises shriek and sigh when they are caught. I have often seen this. They also come to the surface when a storm threatens.

Middle: I often find illustrations of dolphins, and this is how they are illustrated in the *Palace of Animals*, from which I have copied the text below.

Upper right: These look more like mermaids than dolphins.

Lower right: There are no dolphins among us; some people claim that our porpoises are dolphins.

Delphinus is a monster in the sea and its voice sounds like the sighing of humans. They have eyes on the back and the mouth at the front. That is why they always have the mouth pointing upwards and the eyes downwards to continue their hunt. If a storm is imminent they can be heard snoring. They live 140 years and like to hear music played on the lute, harp, flute and similar instruments. And they are said to lament when they are caught. Dolphins do not have ears, but small holes through which they hear, and they have no nostrils to smell with. Still, they have a keen sense of smell and they sleep so happily on the waters that they play on the surface of the water. And they are very loving towards their children and feed them for a long time. They give birth to fully grown children and they have milk in their breasts with which they feed their young. If one of the dolphins dies, the others come to collect the dead one and take him to the sea bed. There they bury him in the ground so that he will not be eaten by other fish and creatures of the sea. The young are always together like a flock of sheep, and there are two old dolphins who keep an eye on them. Dolphins are very attached to one another, because there was once a king who had caught a dolphin, which was tied up in the harbour where the ships came in. Many other dolphins came there and they cried and wailed as if they were begging pardon for the imprisoned dolphin. When the king saw this, he ordered the dolphin to be released, and his will was done. Dolphins play and show themselves on the surface when a storm is on the way. And they help shipwrecked mariners.

Whales and dolphins do not have external ears, but they do have good hearing. They use sound to communicate with one another and the toothed whales hunt using echolocation. They produce a wide variety of sounds. The song of the male humpback whale is famous; he hangs vertically in the water and sings for hours to attract females. Sperm whales make very loud clicking noises, probably to locate their prey in the deep waters where no sunlight penetrates. Large whales can hear one another over large distances by using very low frequencies. The white whale or beluga is nicknamed the 'sea canary' because of his high-frequency repertory with many different details.

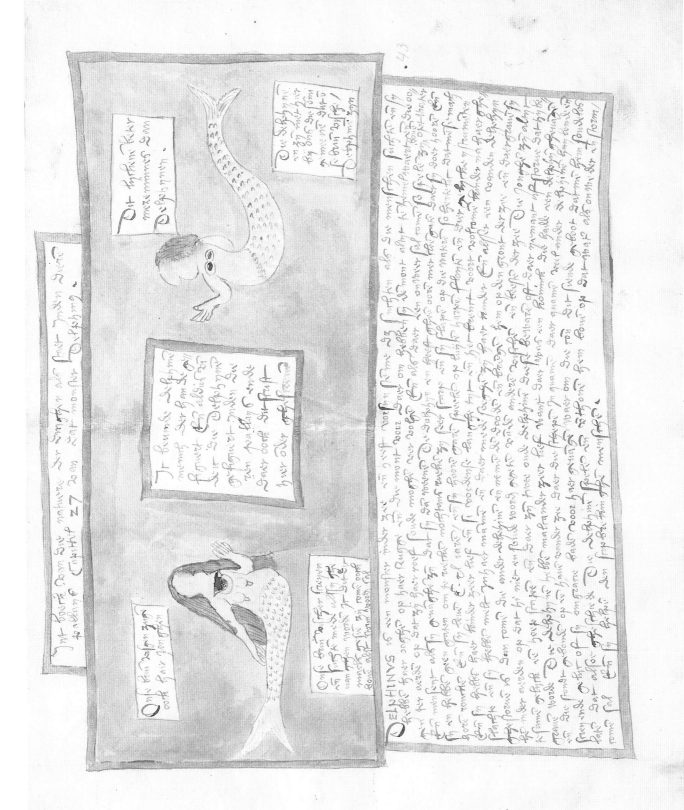

This is roughly what the porpoises among us look like

Centre: A coin on which two dolphins are shown, minted or struck by Alexander the Great. The dolphin is not known among our fishers in Scheveningen, unless the porpoise is a dolphin. That is why what I wrote about the dolphin is taken from other books. Bernard van Breydenbach writes in his book on his journey to the Holy Land as follows: 'On the fourth day of June we were anchored offshore from the city of Parenzo in the galleys waiting for a favourable wind. At that moment we saw very large fish called dolphins which were swimming near the galley. They raced and tumbled cheerfully in the sea for a while like the wheels of a wagon.' The porpoises here among us have the same way of tumbling, as we have often seen here on the coast of Holland.

Pierre Belon writes the following about dolphins: We have seen various ancient coins at the treasurer's with the figure of a curved dolphin, among which I have seen one with the portrait of Alexander the Great. On the other side there were two dolphins curved as below, which shows how much representing the dolphin in this way is contrary to nature. One should not think that the painted dolphin illustrated below shows the truth, but it has been invented by ancient painters and sculptors to show the principal and most admirable feature of the dolphin, which is that when a storm is on its way, it makes great leaps, sometimes passing above a vessel, and in leaping it looks curved in a semicircle like a stick thrown in the air, but in fact it is not curved like that in the water and it is not in the nature of any fish to swim like that.

Bernard van Breydenbach, dean of Mainz Cathedral (*d.* 1497), who travelled to the Holy Land in 1484, wrote an account of his journey in Latin, *Peregrinatio in terram sanctam*. It was published in Mainz in 1486 with 25 woodcuts by the artist Erhard Reuwich, who had accompanied Breydenbach on his pilgrimage.

The images of the leaping dolphin and of the coin are both taken from Pierre Belon. The treasurer is Jean Grolier de Servières, vicomte d'Aguisy (1479–1565), who was government treasurer to François I of France.

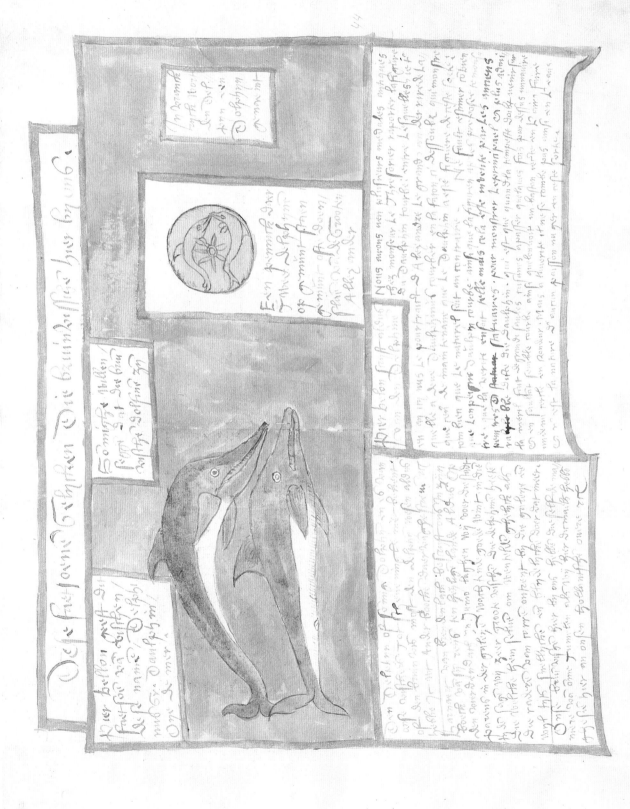

Delphinus

The old dolphins care for the young.
Dolphins bury their dead in the sand.
Dolphins like leaping by nature.

In France near Narbonne the dolphins help the fishers. There is a lot written about this in my *Big Fish Book*. In assisting the fishers they know how to inspect the nets and to jump over them. Dolphins eat bread soaked in wine. That is, when the dolphins have helped the fishers, when they return the next day the fishers give them bread soaked in sweet wine as well as fish. For more about very wondrous things connected with dolphins see my *Big Fish Book*, 1584.

A famous case of fishers being assisted by dolphins is that of the Imraguen fishermen in the north of Mauritania. Yellow mullet are caught with the help of bottlenose dolphins. The dolphins drive the mullet to the coast and feast on them. Afterwards the fishers wade into the water and hang out their nets. The mullet leap out of the water to escape, while the dolphins keep their distance and play with the remaining mullet. Today the mullet is over-exploited and this unusual cooperation is rarely observed.

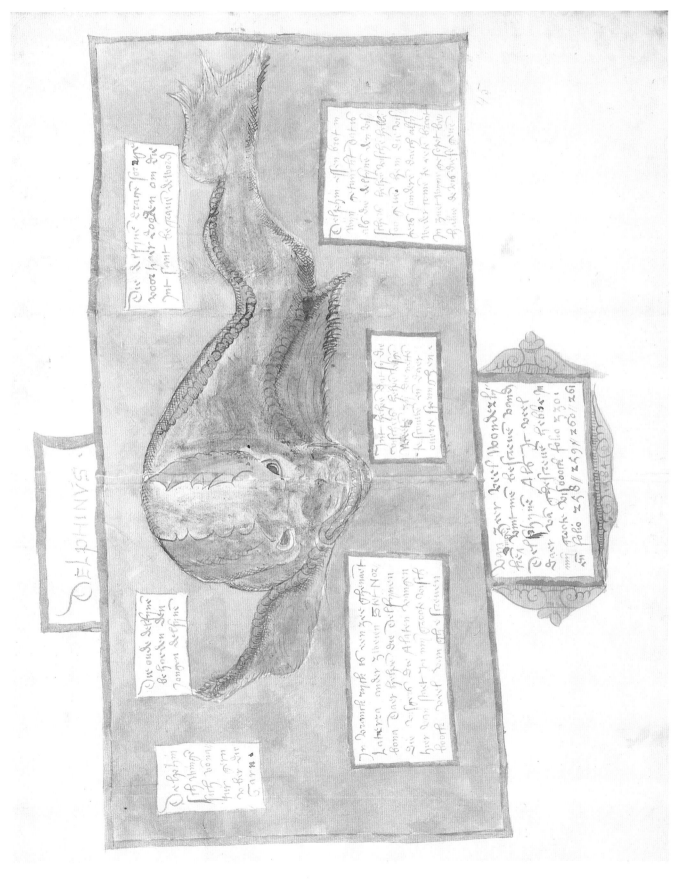

On the famous harpist Arion

Herodotus Book I. When the famous harpist Arion of Methymna had spent a long time in Corinth at the court of Periander, he was seized by a strong urge to sail to France and Sicily, where he managed to accumulate a lot of money and valuables. When he wanted to return home, however, he did not trust foreigners, but only his fellow countrymen, so he took the same boat on which he had come. When they were in the open sea and the Corinthians had discovered that he had money and treasures with him, they made a plan to strangle him and to become masters of his treasure. When Arion discovered this, he surrendered the entire treasure to them and begged them only to be left alive. But the mariners refused and gave him the following choice: if he strangled himself, they would give him a decent burial; otherwise he must jump straight into the sea. Since Arion realized that he had no chance against their superior number, he asked as an only favour to be able to put on his best clothes and to sing a little song and to play the harp. Afterwards he would turn his hand against himself. After he had been playing for a while large dolphins gathered around the ship. One of them kindly received Arion and brought him to the shore near Taenarum, where he climbed off the dolphin and hastened in his best clothes to Corinth. He told Periander all that had befallen him. The latter could hardly believe him. He summoned the mariners to him when they arrived in Corinth, hid Arion, and asked the mariners whether they hadn't seen Arion. When they replied that Arion was still alive and well, travelling in France and enjoying himself there, Arion appeared wearing his familiar clothes. The mariners were dumbstruck and didn't know how to make amends.

The earliest source to recount the story of Arion and the dolphin is the fifth-century BC Ionian historian Herodotus (*Histories*, 1.24).

VANDEN VOORMAELS LIEPE MAER ARION

About a dolphin that brought a lot of fish to a poor woman

Aelian tells that an old woman lived by the water who had a young servant who always gave the dolphin bread. The dolphin reciprocated by bringing the old woman and the boy a lot of fish from its catch every day, so that the woman and the boy lived on that. After the boy died the dolphin was never seen again. There is more on this in my *Fish Book*.

In the time of the Emperor Augustus a dolphin fell in love with the son of a poor man. When the boy went to school in Puteoli and came to the sea in the afternoon, he always called the dolphin by the name of Simon, threw him pieces of bread that he had brought for that purpose, and lured him closer. More on this in my *Fish Book*.

Aelian only mentions the dolphin enamoured with the boy at Puteoli in passing (*On Animals*, 8.15). His account of an elderly couple and their son who feed a dolphin and later receive food in return is in *On Animals*, 11.6.

There are many known cases of dolphins displaying curiosity about humans. Wild dolphins swim among the bathers in Monkey Mia, Western Australia. Amble-on-the-Sea, near the Farne Islands off the coast of Northumberland, had its locally known curious dolphin in the late 1980s. A more recent example is the dolphin George, a regular visitor to the coast near Dorset in the summer of 2002, who later turned up on the Belgian coast displaying a similar interest in humans.

The device with the dolphin

Left: The dolphin who bears the world on its back, enclosed in a ring with a diamond (the old device of the house of the Medici) and a waxing moon (device of King Henry) from which two branches sprout, one of a palm tree as a sign of victory, and one of an olive tree as a sign of coming peace. With these words 'Pacatum / ipse regam avitis virtutibus orbem' will I indicate the noble descent of the king dolphin from father's and mother's side, whereby the waxing moon indicates the nobility of his blood and the diamond his devoutness and invincible might in the world, which is indicated by the globe, just as the ancient Romans rendered it on their coins.

Centre: It appears that Emperor Titus Vespasianus had the anchor with the dolphin as his device, and Pope Paul III the chameleon with a dolphin, by which he referred to the slow haste or ripeness that should be followed in all important matters.

Right: Instead of Augustus' seastar and lobster, Emperor Vespasianus had his coins bear a dolphin with an anchor as you see here.

In other countries, so we find, there are many wonders to be written about dolphins, and people have a lot to do with them. We note that they depict the dolphins in an unusual way.

Coenen's text and image on the device with the dolphin are taken from a work on heraldry: Claude Paradin, *Devises heroïques* (Lyon, 1557). It was published in both French and Dutch (as *Princelijcke Deuisen*) in Antwerp in 1562–3. An English translation of the same work was published in London in 1591. The Latin text means: 'I will rule the pacified world through the virtues of my ancestors'.

A puffer

With a smooth skin without scales.

This big fish was depicted in Frankfurt. Usually the skin of this fish is removed, it is stuffed with cotton, and then sold abroad. They are also hung in apothecaries' and other places as decoration. He has a wide mouth with four wide teeth and is not eaten.

The lumpsucker (*Cyclopterus lumpus*) is 30 to 40 centimetres long and has a smooth skin. It used to be thought that it lived on the sea bed, but in 1983 it was discovered that adult lumpsuckers are also to be found in surface waters. Lumpsuckers off the Dutch coast live close to the sea bed, especially in winter when it is breeding time. The male defends the eggs fanatically. Young lumpsuckers are found from October to June.

Coenen returns to the lumpsucker in Book 2.

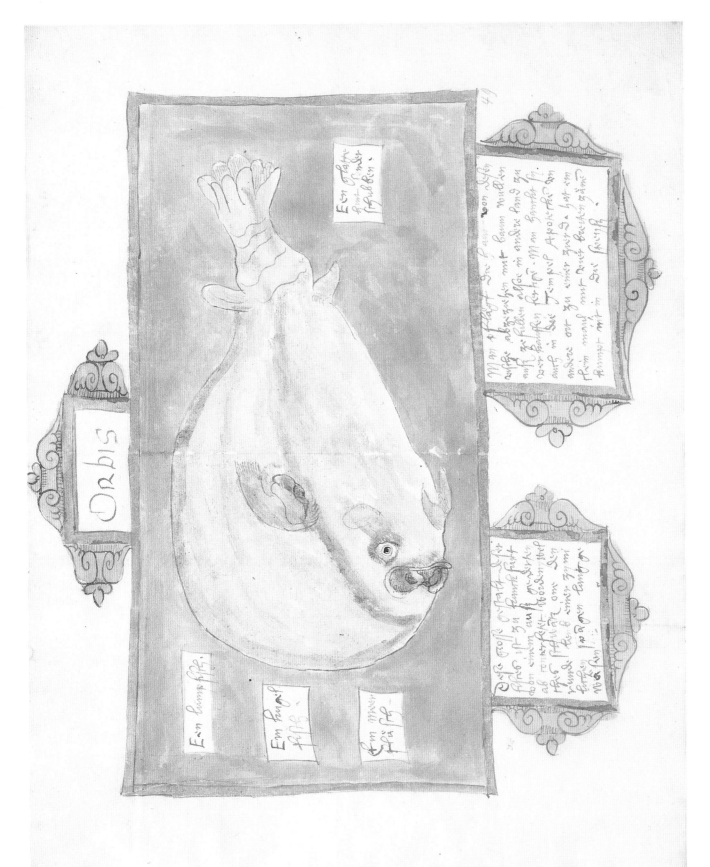

103

This fish was shown in Leiden for money

This fish was caught on 6 September 1581 in Katwijk. He was displayed for money. Afterwards Cornelis Claes, steward in Leiden, bought him and he is still there.

This fish was not familiar to the fishers. The tail and fins were as red as coral and he was the size of a turbot. He had a smooth body like a shiny tin bowl, and the marks were as beautiful and smooth as silver. This fish is offered in temples to the gods by the fishers because of its beauty. The fishers think that in doing so they are rendering the gods a great service. He is called a sacred fish in other countries because of his beauty.

The colourful opah (*Lampris guttatus*) can reach a length of 185 centimetres and a weight of 200 kilograms. It is found between the depths of 100 and 400 metres and is a regular summer visitor to the northern waters of the North Sea. It is a fish of the high seas.

All these fish and little fish are tasty, with a flavour roughly like the herring, but the herring king tastes like gurnard

The *masbancker* is bigger than the common herring and roughly the size of a mackerel. They are caught together with the herring. The fishers smear their hose with the fat that the *masbancker* has in his body, but the ones caught on the coast are a bit less fatty.

Plaskens are caught in the Maas in fresh water. They are tasty when fried. They are smaller than herrings and somewhat broader.

Esselingen taste like these *plaskens*, they are ready as soon as you start to cook them. They are caught in the IJssel. In Zwolle the fishers' children walk with them in the street and call 'come and get *esselingen*, come and get *esselingen*'.

The herring king is very red, like the gurnard, and has scales. There is plenty that could be written about the herring. Everybody is familiar with him,

He is a king of royal might
Who always travels by day and night.
He has no castle, has no fort,
In heaven, earth or hell has nought.
No heathen nor Christian, but well recall,
He is a friend to one and all.

Everyone wants him dead or alive
So many people after him strive.
He costs us Christians many a life
Lamented by both child and wife.

The *pelser* can barely be distinguished from the herring, but he has more guts in his body and is oilier and fatter; he has many scales.

The mackerel is tastier fresh than salted. The Germans write that the mackerel and the *masbancker* are of the same kind as the tunny, which is a tasty fish. I agree with them.

The *blieken* are small fish or young herrings, but nevertheless it seems to be a different sort. They look like the types of fish which the English dry as sprats and the Spaniards salt as sardines.

The *smelten* are somewhat longer than the *blieken* and more slender than the *sparling*, with a skin like the *bliek* or the herring and a flavour like a *plasken*. Our shrimp-fishers catch them close to the shore in their nets.

The *masbancker* is the horse mackerel (*Trachurus trachurus*). The herring king may refer to the oarfish (*Regalecus glesne*), a deep-sea fish 5 to 7 metres long, but this remains unclear from Coenen's text. Herring fishing was one of the mainstays of the Dutch economy in the sixteenth century; Dutch herring fishers were active in the North Sea, the Atlantic and the Zuiderzee, an important breeding ground for herring and anchovy. Gutting was discovered in the fourteenth century, but in the sixteenth century most herring in the Netherlands was not salted but dried or smoked. Most of Coenen's fellow countrymen in Scheveningen will have had facilities to dry fish. Herring has to be salted within 24 hours. Salting on board was not introduced to the Dutch herring fisheries until the seventeenth century, when more salt became available. This made it possible to go on longer voyages without the fish rotting.

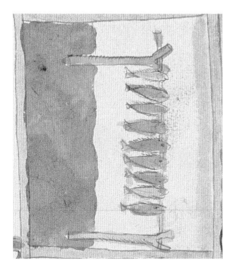

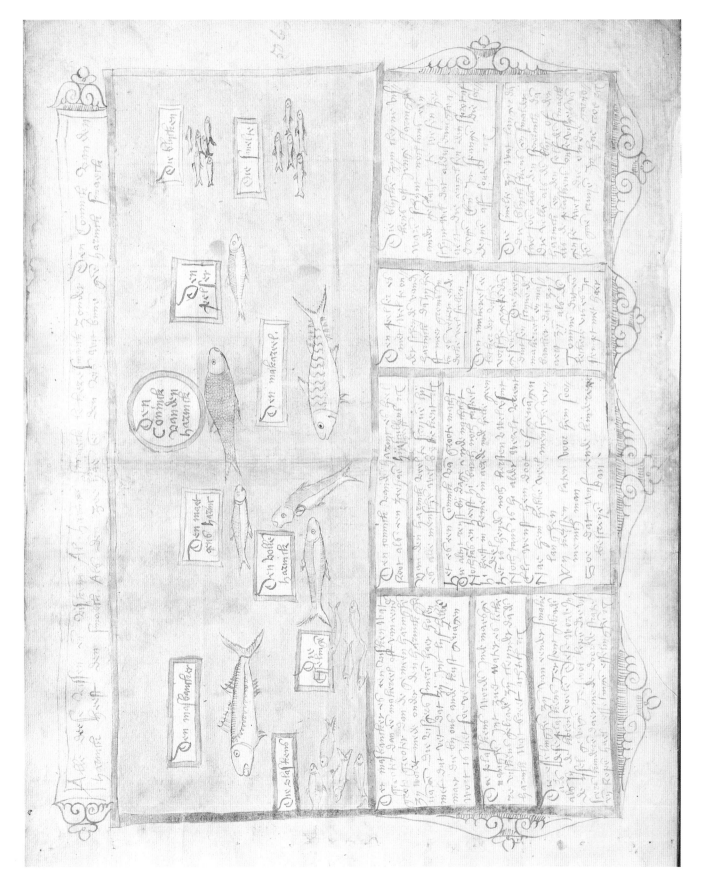

About something strange and wondrous to hear

It happens every year, usually once or twice, sometimes more often. A large group of big fish pass by our village of Scheveningen, coming from the north, and they all trek westwards following the same course past the land, and they leap out of the water – some of them emerge completely from the water, others only half, and they look as if they are chasing one another. When we stand there on the coast near our village this is what we see, and that is how they pass all the villages shown here.

Our fishers say about this: 'They are looking for a bride'; and this was a saying among us when I was a boy, and still is; we don't have anything else to say about it. Our fishers call them *potshooflden* and *wilde bleijen*. We see these fish in such numbers, as far as we can see in a northward, westward and southward direction, that it is impossible to count them. It lasts about two hours and we've never seen them come back in the opposite direction. It usually takes place when the weather is fair and calm, but that trek is almost always followed within three days by a big storm and tempest. We are so used to it here that we don't find it anything unusual, but the people who sometimes come in large numbers from the towns inland find it a very rare and wondrous happening. I note that things like this happen in other countries too: when the big fish leap and trek like this, a storm usually follows soon afterwards.

Oh, how great and good is almighty God in his works: in this way he warns the fishers that a storm is approaching. Almighty God warns the seamen by means of these dumb beasts. That is how I understand it, and may our great God almighty be praised and honoured through Jesus Christ Our Lord and the Holy Ghost, now and for ever more. Amen. Amen. Amen.

It is common knowledge that whales migrate. The best known is the migration of the grey whale (*Eschrichtius robustus*) in the eastern Pacific. Every year they migrate more than 7,500 kilometres along the American coast from Alaska to the west coast of Mexico, where they mate and the calves are born in protected bays. A couple of months later they set out for their feeding grounds in (sub-) arctic waters.

Almost all baleen whales migrate to cold waters in the summer, where the brief but intensive growth of algae guarantees them plenty of food. They start out on the return journey with the approach of winter. It is noteworthy that the winter locations of fin whales are still largely unknown. These enormous creatures are thus capable of hiding away for a part of the year.

What I heard about these big fish and their trek from the President of Holland, Cornelis Suys, Lord of Rijswijk etc. while I sat at his table

How the Prince of Orange, Count William our Stadholder of Holland, and the President of Holland were together in Petten near the Honds Bos and saw the trek of these fish, as I describe it here in the words of the President himself.

It happened that I, Adriaen Coenen of Scheveningen, who write this was on very good terms with the President of Holland, Mr Cornelis Suys, Lord of Rijswijk, and often dined with him when I was in The Hague. For I had made a big book about all kinds of fish which greatly pleased Milord the President and which he liked to discuss and was very curious about. This book was often in his house, and when I went to dine with him, we studied and discussed after the meal with other gentlemen who were often guests there about all kinds of fish, such as the Lord of Oosterwijk who could tell a lot about the fish in Italy. Milord the President greatly enjoyed those discussions about fish with me, because I praised our Dutch fish as delicate while he favoured the Italian fish. I showed that here we throw away as inedible the very fish that he had regarded in Italy as good and delicate, such as the sepia, which is called the sea-cat by us, and the sharks and other fish. This took place at the time when I was on good terms with the President, before the troubles with the Beggars.

Once I was dining there and while we were talking about the fish – whereby he usually asked (now about this one, now about another fish) whether they were in my book – Milord the President told me how he had once been in Petten near the Honds Bos, which people are always working on and which involves huge expense. As he said, the Stadholder of Holland, the Prince of Orange, was also there. While they sat at table, people came to tell them that a large group of big fish had arrived from the east and passed the coast heading westward. They jumped out of the water as they chased one another. We left our table to go and see and we noted that that was the case. He also told me that they then summoned a few old men and asked them what it meant. The old men replied: 'the fish are going to find a bride' and 'this happens more often, and we fishers have an old saying for it: they are looking for a bride'. Then I said: 'Sire, this often happens near us off the coast near our village of Scheveningen,' as I have described it in my *Fish Book*, which was in his house at the time. And Milord the President was able to say a lot about it, including the fact that they jump out of the water. After he had finished his story, Milord asked: 'Didn't the old men say any more about that?' 'No,' Milord replied. And I said: 'Among us people say that it is usually followed within three days by a storm and tempest.' At which Milord the President said: 'That is true. When we had left Petten and I and the Prince of Orange were on our way to Amsterdam and we were on the dyke between Haarlem and Amsterdam, the wind started to blow so violently that it scared us and we were afraid of being blown off the dyke, coach and all.'

That is what Milord the President told me and my book was in his house at the time (as it very often was). They fetched my book and I showed those present what I had written about the trek of these big fish. What I had described was exactly what the President had seen and heard. This saying 'to search for the bride' existed when I was a boy and is still in use now that I am an old man. When I wrote this I was over 70. This is enough about that.

The Egmond whale, 1547
[for illustration see following two pages]

This is the image of the fish that was stranded in Egmond on 8 May 1547. This fish lay on his back with his belly turned upwards. The belly was mottled, white and black; the back was black.

From one jaw to the other it was 16 feet long and the jaws were 10 feet wide; from navel to tail 25 feet long; the tail was 16 feet wide. This whole fish was 75 feet long (of 11 thumbs per foot) and 38 feet wide. From the eye to the nose it was 14 feet, and from the eye to the fin 6 feet. The fin itself was 6 feet.
Above: These are the monks in Egmond.

Coenen is here referring to the famous abbey of Egmond, one of the great abbeys that influenced Dutch politics and culture.

This drawing is of a large fin whale (*Balaenoptera physalus*), a species surpassed in size only by the blue whale. This smaller relative can still attain a length of 24 metres. It occurs in all oceans. Stranded fin whales are fairly rare in the Netherlands and Belgium. At least three cases were reported on the Belgian coast in 1939, 1978 and 1997. A 12-metre fin whale crashed into a landing stage in Flushing in January 2001 and died afterwards. A 15-metre fin whale spent some time in the Westerschelde in June 2002 before heading back to open water.

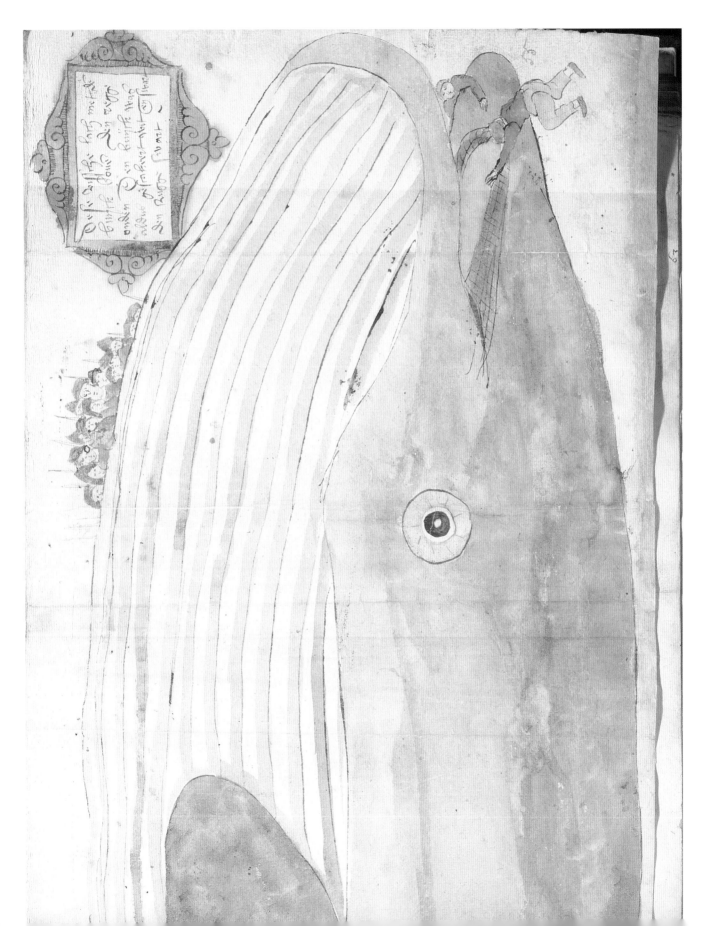

Good viewer and reader: here you have seen many strange and big, wondrous fish.
Herein can one see the wondrous works of God almighty be praised.

The Second Book

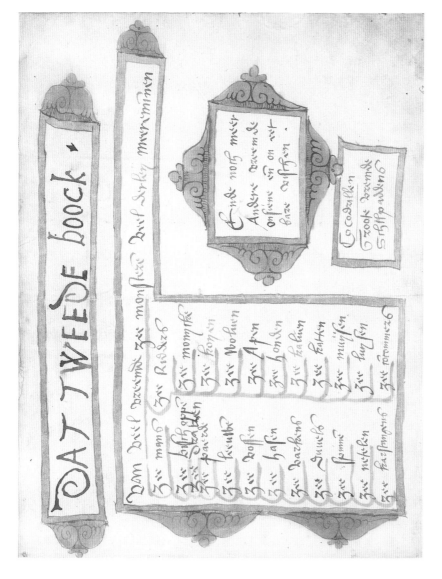

About many strange sea monsters, all kinds of mermaids, mermen, sea knights, sea bishops, sea monks, sea dragons, sea cows, sea horses, sea wolves, sea lions, sea monkeys, sea foxes, sea dogs, sea hares, sea calves, sea swine, sea cats, sea devils, sea mice, sea spiders, sea lice, sea nettles, sea cucumbers, sea chestnuts and yet more about other strange unknown and inedible fish, such as crocodiles and large strange tortoises.

The Brazilian sea monster

Its skin was 17 feet long.

What a wonder! In December 1564 this monster was seen on the bank of the river, three or four fathoms out of the water, near the house of George Ferrara in Brazil near St Vincent in the city of Santos. It uttered loud cries as it rolled over with pleasure in the undergrowth beside the river. Balthasar Ferrara, a young man and George's son, approached the monster with a sword and when it saw him, it fled to the sea or the water, whereby it dropped into the water and slipped down through the water-plants. The young man struck the monster a blow in the head from the bank of the river. The wounded monster cried out loudly and rose upright on its feet, which looked like those of a goose. The young man saw that it did not flinch, but aimed his sword and struck the monster with it. Then the locals killed this monster with bows and arrows. Its skin or hide was as soft as the most fluffy velvet, which cannot be described. The likeness of this monster was sent to the King of Portugal and the skin is expected to be sent there.

The story of the Brazilian monster also appeared in Coenen's first *Fish Book* and in the *Big Fish Book*. The narrative in the *Big Fish Book* and in the *Whale Book* is the same, but the accompanying illustrations are different. The episode is illustrated in a copper-plate engraving by Jerónimo Luiz in *Historia da provincia Sancta Cruz a qui vulgarmente chamamos Brasil by Pedro de Magalhães de Gandavo* (Lisbon, 1576). Coenen's source, however, is a German pamphlet, *Newe Zeytung von einem seltzamen Meerwunder [...]*, published in Augsburg by M. Franck.

It has been suggested that the creature in question is a sea cow or manatee (*Trichechus manatus*), but a sea cow cannot leave the water and stand upright. Coenen may have depicted a fur seal. Fur seals can stand upright and their flippers could be described as the feet of a goose. Given the size of this creature, it may have been a South American fur seal (*Arctocephalus australis*), which is also found today in Brazil. The male fur seal has a thickly maned fur and can be as long as 2.8 metres. Fur seals have an extremely soft and velvety fur.

117

Circhos, Tigris

Left: About the fish *circhos* from the *Palace of Animals* chapters 24 and 22.
Right: About the *tigris* from the *Palace of Animals* chapter 97.

Circhos is a beast of the sea and on its skin it has hard shells, black and in some places red.
It has four feet – the left large, the right small – and three toes on each foot. When it moves
it supports itself mainly on the left foot. If there is a storm and the wind gets up, it creeps
under the stones. It is strong when the weather is fine, but ill when the weather is poor. It
has a head like a human and a lower body like a seal.

Tigris is a beast of the sea that always bears its young in the water and not on the water.
Sometimes they come out of the water, when a north wind blows, and then it is half-blind
in the left eye. These creatures follow the ships out of curiosity, because they want to see the
sails on the ships. They become so fat that they usually die in their third or fourth year. In
Ethiopia there are beasts called *tigri*, and they have a yellow colour and two breasts on the
upper body with which they suckle their young.

TIGRVS
TIGRVI.

Turbot

Van Thigrus in Tigrui als fart
onden zwo falug 6 jut 27 Capittel

Van den difft Turtot 6 als fart
onden zwo falug Cap. 24 c 222.

Een beest der zee is Tigrus in beent
alhyt hyn honde deest in dat water, en mit op
dat water een dyere fom hyp en dat marstab
dec neede zunt abant en dan it hillet geset
andere lieffer wossy fin in zee der soote de
syste zt niein on dat dy die zeyte zunde
master zit op die dyere Och bieffen weden,
zoe niet dat hy niet koment zynt deelde op
in Ethiopien fyn diefs Tigru Ofte
beede in die zoeken en lieffer die die zunde
deese mannen hangende zee die barst zwezffy
zaer wondt mede lucett

Turtbos is een beest der zee zee in heeft
dat hooft geset lichtet mit fief
op fruit en of fom die liesffen wel
en beest en loeken die lieffer boet
zygrosst in die zehler wel zwen zy
anderzont zeue zn ziemyzee en alt
dat die feangst fin meest die lieffen
roeken En alt onther die wunde op
dat zoo koet onde die frezen
in zoos weet it beet in onthe die
it zeer Gefuell von boet als in
mens fin en dat ander bep als syn
zee bout.

Mermen, mermaids, nereids

Left: About a man and a woman who showed themselves in the River Nile. In 1570 two human figures appeared in the Nile up to the navel, a man and a woman; the other half of the body was under water. They had long hair and could be seen from morning to noon.

Centre: I come across all kinds of renderings of mermaids and mermen in writings, and they are described in many books. But I have never found or seen a person in the whole course of my life who has seen a merman or mermaid with his own eyes. When I wrote this I was 70 years old, in the year of Our Lord 1584.

Right: Chapter 54 of the *Palace of Animals* states on the Nereids that they are sea monsters with coarse hair on their bodies and that they look somewhat like humans. If one of them is about to die, he laments and wails with a loud human voice, so that it can be heard from afar.

Siren

Chapter 83 of the *Palace of Animals* states that sirens are mermaids, deadly creatures that like to kill people. From the head to the navel they resemble women, they are very large with a terrible appearance and have very long, dirty and slimy hair. The rest of the body is like an eagle, and has feet with claws with which they tear their prey, and a tail with scales like a fish. They sing a sort of delightful song by which they entice sailors towards them, and when the sailors hear this song it usually sends them to sleep, and then the mermaids come and drag the sailors out of their ships and rip them apart. But wise sailors block their ears to prevent them from hearing this song. These sirens carry their young with them in their arms and suckle them with their big breasts at the front of their upper bodies. If sailors see mermaids darting on the water, they are already in difficulty, and once the mermaids approach the ships, the sailors cast out empty barrels with which they play until the ships have passed. This is what I was told by those who have seen it. There are also a few places in Arabia where there are large serpents that are also called sirens; they run faster than a horse and have large wings to fly.

The siren makes its first appearance in Book 12 of the *Odyssey* of Homer. In medieval bestiaries it is depicted as half woman and half fish, or half woman and half bird.

The real-life sirens are the sea cows in the taxonomic order *Sirenia*. They are notorious herbivores, moving gently through fields of sea grass. Four species are still in existence. A fifth, the giant Steller's sea cow, existed in small numbers in the North Pacific, but was hunted to extinction between 1743 and 1763.

Sea bishop; about a wondrous monster that was caught in 1431

Bishops are not the only ones on earth
That are held to be of great worth.
There is a sea bishop too, a tough biter,
Who does not speak though he wears a mitre.

In 1431 a fish was caught in the kingdom of Poland that was as long and broad as a living bishop and decorated with a mitre, staff, white chasuble, stole, maniple, shoes, hems, gloves and all the other requisites that correspond to the dignity of a bishop. Further this fish had a head, eyes, ears, forehead, nose, mouth, cheeks, shoulders, arms, hands and feet and all other limbs exactly like a grown man or bishop. In front and behind his chasuble was raised to the knees, but to the touch he felt like a cold living fish. He allowed all kinds of people, and especially the bishops of that country, to touch him. When this fish and bishop was presented to the King of Poland and was asked in all kinds of languages who he was and where he came from, he did not reply. However, he opened his mouth and humbly paid his respects to the bishops present. The king was furious because he would not speak and intended to have him thrown into the dungeons, at which this fish and bishop was greatly saddened. He closed his eyes and did not want to open them again. Then the bishops of the country fell on their knees in the presence of the king and begged him to send the fish back to the coast of the sea where he had been caught. The Lord God, whose works are unfathomable, would reveal the nature and meaning of this so that no plagues or sorrow should ensue for the king and his subjects. When the king gave his assent, the fish immediately opened his eyes again and showed the king and the bishops in particular great gratitude. Then a cart was prepared in the presence of innumerable people, on which the bishops sat down with this fish and bishop. The fish sat reasonably and well-manneredly among them like a rational being. When they were still a fairly long way off, they got out of the cart to cover the last part of the journey on foot. The fish did the same, stood upright on his feet, and walked between two bishops, with one hand on the shoulder of one bishop and the other on that of the other, like a reasonable, living creature. He was not bothered or affected by the large numbers of people, but proceeded in a well-mannered way like the other bishops. When he reached the sea, he gave the bishops and the people a friendly look. He humbly took leave of the bishops with great

124

Both Rondelet and Gessner, who give the date 1531, neither affirm nor deny the existence of the sea bishop.

The *Dutch Chronicle* is the *Chronicle of Holland, Zeeland and Friesland* by Cornelius Aurelius, a monk from Gouda, which Coenen here copies verbatim. This chronicle, first published in Leiden in 1517, went through 53 editions between 1538 and 1802. It was in turn based on an earlier Latin chronicle by Johannes à Leydis.

reverence, bowed, and asked for permission to leave. At that he entered the water alone, gave the bishops a hand, and when the water was up to his navel and he began to feel the depth, he was delighted and turned to face the people and the bishops. He bowed his head very low to the people and blessed them with his right hand, with which he made the sign of the Holy Cross, as though he was a real ard genuine bishop. Then he swam away and was never seen again. This wonder was seen by a famous doctor who tells it, considering it to be true. And if this really is true, then one can see in it the wondrous works of God almighty, that are unfathomable, may he be praised now and for ever. Amen.

Conrad Gesner who made a big fish book writes that there are sea bishops, but he does not write much about them. I have taken the above from the *Dutch Chronicle*.

A sea monk

The sea gives us fish in plenitude
To the Lord we show our gratitude
But it surely is a strange affair
That monks like these can be found there.

Pierre Belon writes on sea monsters: Just as the land produces all kinds of wondrous creatures, so should one not doubt that the sea (which is much larger and is full of innumerable fishes and other marine creatures) produces all kinds of monsters and strange sorts. Both old and new stories report sirens, tritons, naiads and nereids, just as for the land authors have written about the belief in stories that they have seen fauns and satyrs. If one may attach credence to the writings and recollections of Pliny, then in that time various nobles at sea saw a merman walking over the ships at night and sinking some of them, after which he plunged back into the sea. Not so long ago a merman was seen in Norway by countless people; he was covered with fish scales, walked along the edge of the water, and was enjoying himself sunbathing.

In the *Annals of Brabant* is found a fish in the form of a bishop covered with scales, with his mitre and his pontifical adornments, who was caught near Poland and sent to the king of that country in 1531, as is written by Cornelius of Amsterdam to a Mr Gilbert, a Roman physician. This same Cornelius writes that, during the great floods in his country, a female monster was found in a lake and taken to the town of Edam, who lived for some time with the women of this country, carrying out all the work and activities of a woman, but she never spoke and could not learn a single word. Another marine monster or fish was found in Norway near the town of Denelopoch in the country of Dieze, having the figure of a monk in the form that you will see painted below. This monster, which was seen by several people, did not live more than three days and could not speak, but only uttered deep sighs. I can assure you of it by the stories and writings of people worthy of belief and do not find anything in that which nature cannot bring about, just like several other things that we experience every day.

In 1403 a 'wild woman' drifted or swam into the Zuiderzee and reached the Purmer-lake through a breach in the dyke. She was completely naked, but covered with a shaggy layer of some watery material. The woman was captured and taken to Edam. Later people paid to see her on show in Haarlem, where she learnt how to spin and lived for many years. Her story, taken from the *Dutch Chronicle*, is told in both of Coenen's manuscripts.

Both Belon and Rondelet include woodcuts of the sea monk and sea bishop. The latter claimed to have received an image of the sea monk from Marguerite de Valois, Queen of Navarre, and to have obtained confirmation from a certain Gisbertus Germanus, a physician in Rome.

The monk seal (*Monachus monachus*), found in the eastern Mediterranean and off the coast of West Africa, may owe its name to its complexion or to the thick layer of fat around the neck, which looks like a folded monk's cap. Many local names for this mammal in the Mediterranean refer to the monk. Today it is one of the rarest mammals in the world, with an estimated population of less than 500.

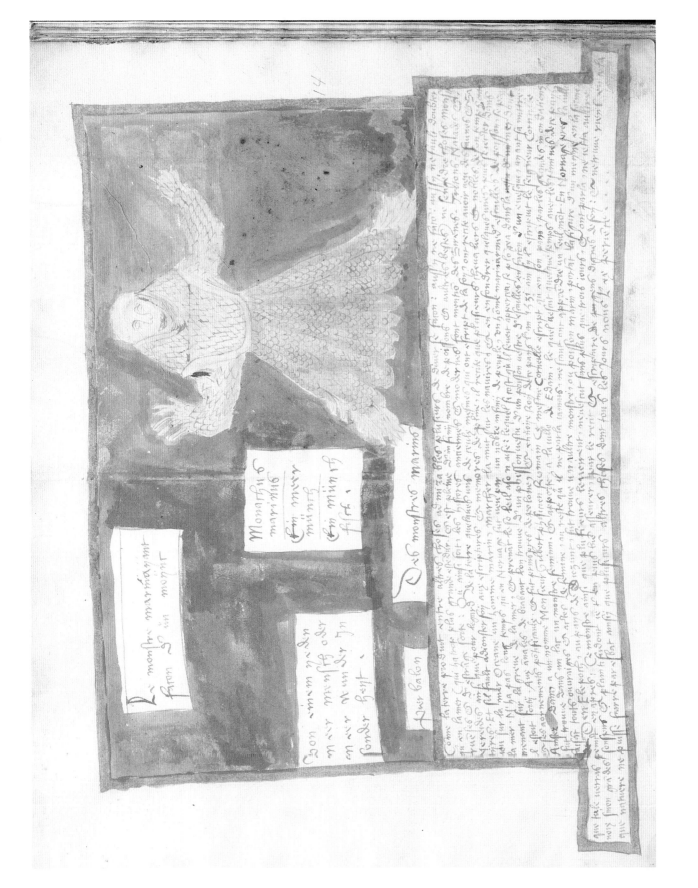

About sea dragons

Left: Draco marinus. When a sea dragon is caught and brought to land, he very skilfully digs a hollow in the sand with his beak and hides in it.

Albertus: The sea dragon uses its feathers to swim; it covers a large distance in a short time.

Centre: As it is written in the *Palace of Animals.* Leviathan is a Hebrew word and means dragon. He walks on the land, swims in the water and flies in the air. This dragon often fights with the whale. All fish in the sea that see this fight head immediately for the tail of the whale, and if the whale is beaten by the dragon and dies, the dragon eats all the fish that are near the tail. But if the dragon is unable to beat the whale, he blows a large quantity of poison in the direction of the whale. When the whale sees this, he takes in a large amount of water and blows it in the direction of the dragon, thereby fending off the poison and saving himself, all his companions and the fish near his tail.

Right: Chapter 26 of the *Palace of Animals* states: The sea dragon is a monster, very cruel and terrible, just like land dragons. He is very long, but has no wings. He has a knotted tail and his skin has hard scales. He crosses a large expanse of water in a short time. Absinthe is a remedy for the bite of the sea dragon.

Leviathan, a sea dragon

Heed what I say:
Leviathan I shall not portray
For after looking in all the books,
That would not be the right way.
Him I may not picture
Otherwise than as in the scriptures.

For as the scholars opine
The work of Leviathan is of the mind,
Not just a dragon or fish of the sea.
Hence his image may not be made by me.

In Job 40 and 41 you will find,
Before these chapters do end,
That Leviathan lives in the swell,
And you will find there as well
His nature, works and art
That strike terror into every heart.

No more than this may I surmise,
I leave it all up to the wise,
To matters such their minds to lend,
Before they reach a perfect end.

On crocodiles in German

Although the crocodile sometimes lives in the water, he contains not water but blood, and breathes air. He has four large forked feet and a long tail but no ears, to prevent the water from entering. He has a tough skin full of ridges and scales.

John Mandeville writes about an island called Silha that is five hundred miles in circumference. There are all kinds of plagues there. There are also many serpents and dragons and crocodiles, so that no one dares to live there. Crocodiles are serpents with four feet, short legs and large claws. Some are five fathoms long, others six or even ten, and when they move through sandy ground, it is as though a large tree is being dragged through the sand. (I who write this once saw the skin of a crocodile in The Hague, which you could pay to see. It had been folded into three pieces. As far as I could see, it was no longer than four fathoms.) John Mandeville writes elsewhere that there are also many crocodiles in all kinds of places in other countries too. At night they live in the water, and in the daytime they live on rocks and in caves. They do not eat in the winter, but lie in their crannies like snakes. This crocodile eats people and weeps as it kills them. When he eats them, he grinds them with his lower and upper jaws.

Chapter 25 of the *Palace of Animals* contains the following: the crocodile has large teeth and claws and his skin is so tough that does not feel anything if people throw large stones at his back. He is yellow and lives in one of the four rivers that flow from Paradise, called the Nile. They lay their eggs in the ground; the male and the female take turns to guard them.

On the nature of crocodiles, caution and moderation in drinking. The crocodile, who knows beforehand how far the flooding of the Nile will extend, lays her eggs in places that will not be inundated. The lesson for us is to avoid imminent peril.

Caution is the mother of wisdom.
Many monsters are bred by the Egyptian land,
And much evil lurks in the waters of the Nile.
'Tis unsafe to drink for any man,
And even the dog does wait a while.
Wise he holds back his panting tongue
To slake his thirst with the cool dip,
He wants no poison to do him wrong,

'Tis enough for him the waters to sip.
Measure in all he does observe
The better his life to preserve.

Much worse are those who do not think
But always fill themselves with drink.
Transformed they are to animal kinds
With human form but thoughtless minds.

Coenen is here drawing on chapters 21 and 31 of the *Travels of Sir John Mandeville* (written in the mid-fourteenth century), which was widely available in printed editions in the sixteenth century. Silha is Sri Lanka.

The crocodile is the 'dinosaur' of the reptiles, estimated to go back 200 million years. The Nile crocodile (*Crocodylus niloticus*) is found in East Africa and in the Nile. There is also a dwarf crocodile (*Ostaeolaemis tetraspis*) in West Africa. There are various crocodile species that also occur in coastal waters.

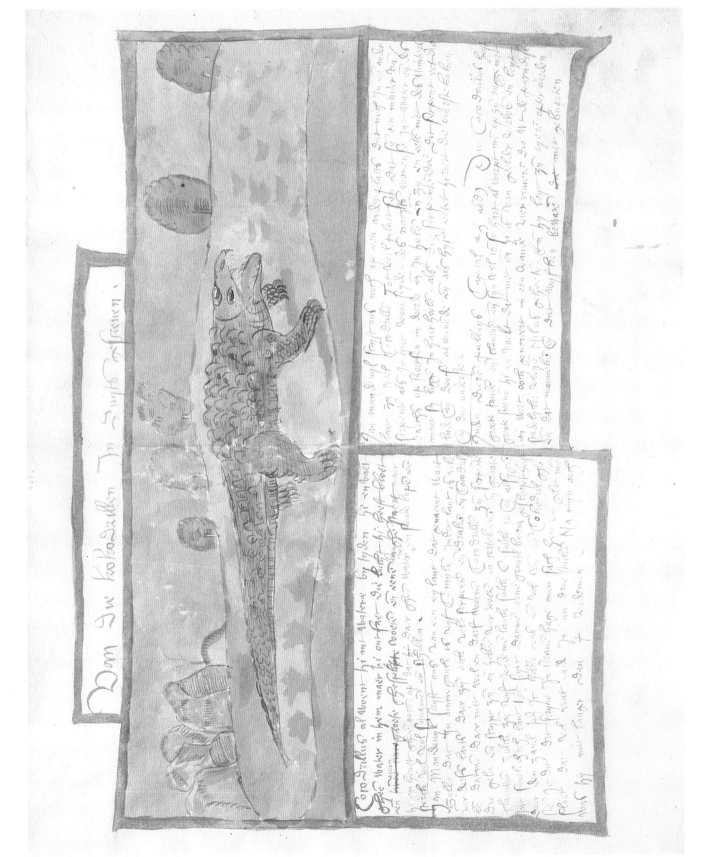

The pharaoh rat, the skink or small crocodile

It is said that when the crocodile sleeps, with his mouth open, a small bird called *Trochilus*, that is *roitelet*, enters his jaws and feeds on what it finds between the teeth. There is a certain kind of rat in this country called ichneumon that even creeps into the crocodile's stomach, and when he has eaten his fill of what he finds there and cannot return by the same route, he eats his way out of the stomach, causing the death of the crocodile. The common people in Egypt call this creature a Pharaoh rat. It does not look at all like the armadillo, but has a tail like a cat, a fairly long body, and a snout like a weasel.

What the ancients called a skink is a sort of land crocodile. Since it is used in medicine and the less skilful apothecaries tend to confuse it, it seems sensible for us to describe all these animals here in order to be able to distinguish them and also to recognize their strange colourings. The first is the skink (which some call a small crocodile), no larger than a salamander, nor thicker than the wrist or longer than a thumb and a half. His skin is black, striped on the back with a deep red colour. He is covered with scales like a fish. He lives both in the water and on land, and in many ways resembles the lizard. The skink is found in Egypt, India and Mauritania near the River Memphis: the merchants there catch it and dry it for sale.

It is interesting to note that Coenen assumes a familiarity on the part of his readers with the armadillo (he illustrated one in his big *Fish Book*, see inset), an animal from the New World that was best known in Europe from the presence of its dried shell in many collections of curiosities. The source for his image is Belon.

Le Rat de Pharaon

Le Smaque ou Arche Crocodylle

Le Siroque

About big tortoises and big snails

In the Indian Ocean the shells of tortoises are so big that the people use them to make houses and boats. They are caught everywhere. The Indians eat these tortoises; they provide good meat, which tastes like veal. Conrad Gesner claims to have seen such creatures in the Black Sea. Their flesh is soft and pleasant to eat.

The people who live beside the Red Sea also use such shells to make small boats in which they sail from one island to another. These tortoises are caught in all kinds of ways, especially when the midday sun drives them to the surface of the sea and they float with their whole back above water. They delight so much in sunbathing and having a breath of fresh air beneath the blue sky that they forget everything and their shell is so dried out by the great heat that they can no longer sink below the surface. So they are left to swim to and fro on the surface and are easy to catch, even by hand. They lay eggs like birds' eggs, about a hundred in number, that they cover with fine sand on the land. They hatch them by sitting on them at night.

In medieval bestiaries the term here translated as 'tortoise' was probably taken to refer to any animal with a shell.

Turtles usually lay their eggs on a beach where the waves break against the shore. They dig a deep hole to allow sufficient humidity for the eggs, lay them in it, and cover them with sand. After many weeks the hatchlings crawl out of the eggs and dig their way up through the sand. This always takes place at night, when they are drawn to the water by the light of the waves breaking. The four circumpolar species that are also found in Europe are the green turtle, the leatherback, the loggerhead and Kemp's Ridley turtle. The largest is the green turtle, whose shell can be a metre long. Turtle species are nowadays endangered, nest sites are destroyed by human activity, and in various countries eggs are still dug up for food.

Some turtle nests are at least 3,000 kilometres from the feeding grounds. One marked leatherback travelled more than 6,000 kilometres in ten months and reached a depth of more than 1,200 metres. The last-known leatherback nest in the Mediterranean was on Sicily in the years 1930–40.

A big tortoise that arrived in Scheveningen in 1565 and all kinds of snails, mussels and shells

On 18 June 1565, Whit Monday, a man in Scheveningen called Frans Jans – who usually spent the whole summer shrimping – grabbed this big tortoise when it came out of the sea and crawled onto the beach. It had a beak like an eagle and wings and fins, and instead of having feet at the back it had flat fins that looked like feet, and a big shell like the tortoises. His head moved in and out. The shell was the size of a barber's bowl. I bought the tortoise from this man for six Carolus guilders and kept him in my home for a long time. Afterwards I sent someone out to show it for money, and he brought it back dead. I disembowelled it and dried it. The intestines were like those of a bird. I had kept him alive for a long time in a bucket of water, but he would not eat. When I had dried him, I gave him to Milord of Moerkercke alias Milord of Renouteren, a nobleman in Flanders. This good lord was a great lover of rare and strange things concerning birds and fish. He had two painters who illustrated rare birds and fish for him every day. He had these painters daily in his court. This good lord entertained me at his table during his stay in The Hague, almost half a year, for a big court case. As this gentleman told me, he had a house in Ghent and in Bruges and other courts and seignories as well as wonderful mazes and gardens about which wondrous tales could be told. Here in The Hague he had a large retinue of servants and six or eight fine stallions and horses, cooks and pages, and a beautiful young wife with her retinue. He was plagued by gout but he was a Latin scholar who greatly loved art and science and was very curious about rare and strange things.

Before that I had once seen such a sea eagle in Delft, and it looked just like the one I have described here. This tortoise in Delft was on show for payment and was alive in a barrel of water. Earlier still I visited the home of a burgomaster in Schiedam who had the shell of a tortoise that had once belonged to a big merchant who traded with distant countries. In this house of burgomaster Tack I saw a big shell of a tortoise or sea eagle hanging. This shell was four times the size of mine and, so I was told, it had been found by fishermen who rowed ashore with a small boat and discovered tortoises there in the dunes and hills sitting on a big pile of eggs, more than a hundred. They grabbed one and took it to the boat with all its eggs, and the shell I saw was from that creature. So there are big tortoises in distant countries.

Snails and mussels are common among us and everyone knows them, so there is no point in writing about them.

Charles de Saint-Omer (1533–1569) was a nobleman and collector of *naturalia* who owned a castle and estate at Moerkercke near Bruges. He was a patron of the famous botanist Carolus Clusius. He brought together the core of the collection of the botanical and zoological watercolours known as *Libri Picturati A.16-30* in the Jagiellonska Library, Kraków.

On the right are the mussel (*Mytilus edulis*) and the common snail (*Cochlea spec.*). It was already known in the fourteenth century that mussels can be caught and then kept in water close to home, where they continue to grow without losing their flavour. This is the basis of modern mussel farming, which 'fattens' small mussels that are fished when they are about 1 centimetre long. Already in the nineteenth century measures had to be taken against over-exploitation of mussels. Mussel farming is still a flourishing industry today.

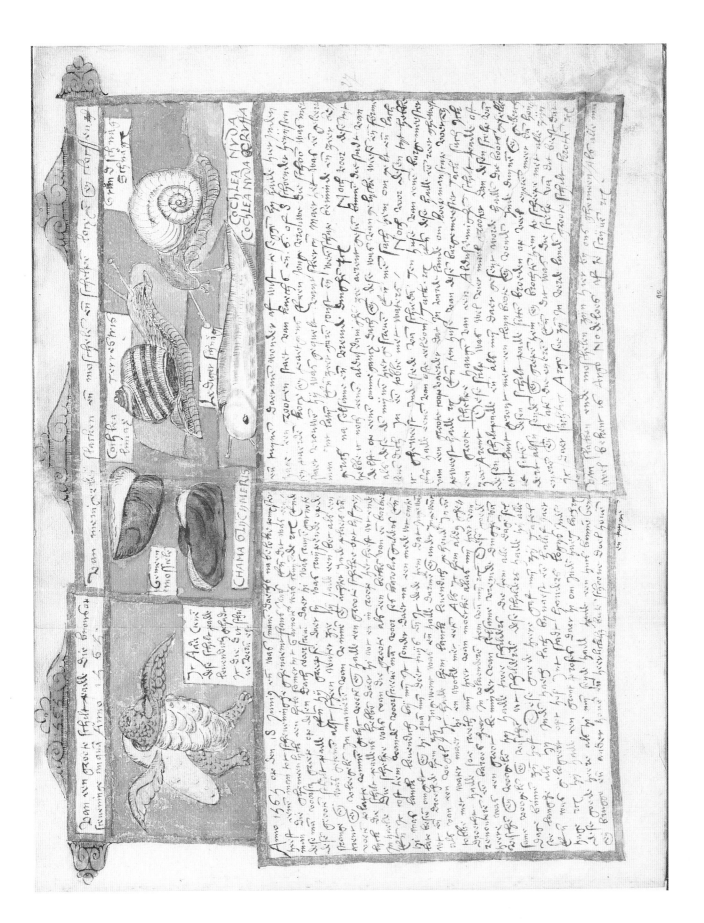

Sea cows, sea calves, sea bulls

The sea calf is a creature with a tough skin, covered with hair and dappled with black and white spots. It gives birth on land and feeds its young with milk and gives them suck. The young are not taken to the water by the mother until they are 12 days old. Almost the only way to kill them is to dash in their brains. This creature sleeps too, and snores with a loud bellow. It is said to place its right fin under its head when it sleeps. When this creature has been skinned, its hair stands on end if the sea is rough and subsides when the sea is calm, and that means ebb and flood.

The *Foca* is a sea ox, very strong, courageous and violent against other animals, including domesticated oxen. He always fights with his partner until he has killed her. Then he finds another wife and stays with her until he dies or is beaten and killed by his wife. He always stays in the place where he was born. He and his children live from theft. This is written in the *Palace of Animals.*

The name Foca refers to the seal. Seals were abundant in the Netherlands and it is remarkable that Coenen does not mention the harbour seal (*Phoca vitulina*). When seals lie on a sandbank, it is easy to see that where their skin is dry, the hairs stand on end and lose their sheen. Coenen's description of the sea calf could be a reference to the seal.

Sea horses

Once when I, Adriaen Coenen, was a young lad and was playing with other lads and friends from Scheveningen in the dunes on the coast, as we were looking for blackberries we emerged from the dunes and saw a lot of people who had come from Scheveningen to see a sea horse that had come close to the shore between Scheveningen and Berckheij, but had swum off again. It had been seen by a man who was passing by, and he had brought the news to Scheveningen. The first to arrive still saw the sea horse swimming out to sea, but it was already gone by the time I reached the shore. This picture of this sea horse was hung on a sign in Delft with the words: 'This is the sea horse that was seen between Berckheij and Scheveningen,' with the date, but I've forgotten it. It had long teeth.

Aristotle: The sea horse is a monster in the East and it looks very wondrous, with its head held high. It has hair like a horse, cloven hooves like a cow, and a tail like a pig. It is the size of a donkey and lives in the water or on land as it chooses.

Hippopotamus is a creature that is born on land but lives in the water too. It is as strong in water as on land and is usually larger than an elephant. It has an upturned jaw and big crooked teeth. This creature seeks its food on land and at night it visits the fields where corn grows, as well as other seeds such as barley, oats, beans, buckwheat and so on. It walks backwards as it eats to see better whether anyone wants to hit or hurt it. This creature lives in the River Nile and especially in some countries in India.

Aristotle says: Although this creature lives on land, it cannot live without water, like the tortoise and the crocodile and other aquatic creatures. Pliny says: The hide of the hippopotamus is so thick and hard that it can be used to make armour.

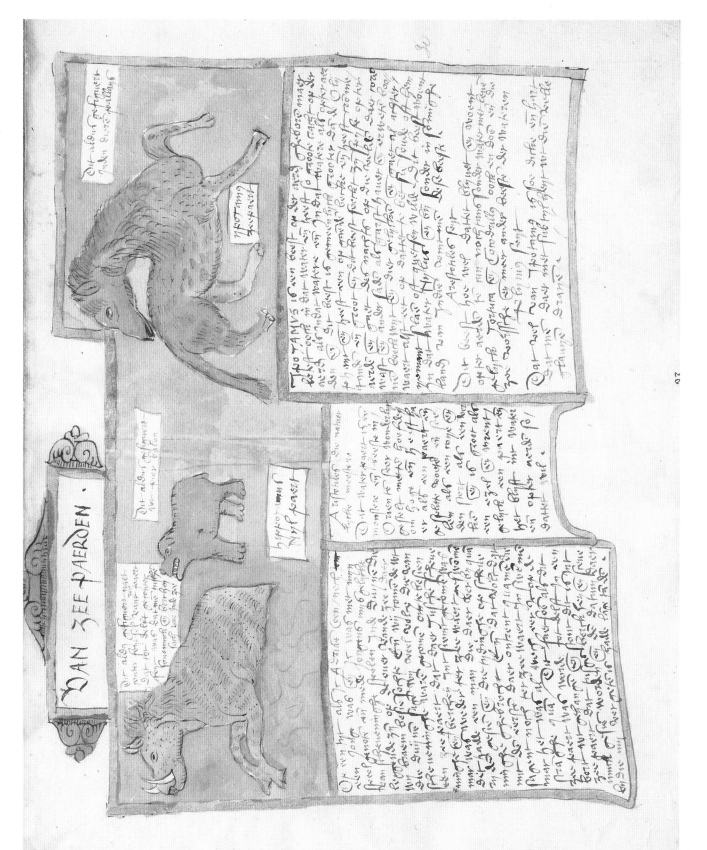

On the river horses that are called hippopotamus, the horse of the Nile

Left: This figure is found minted on a medallion. The portrait of the hippopotamus taken from the reverse of the medallion of the Emperor Hadrian as communicated to us by Monsieur the treasurer Grolier. Described in more detail in my *Big Fish Book*.

Right: The Nilotic river horse, taken from the ancient marble, representing the River Nile which is in Rome in the garden of the Pope's palace. Described in more detail in my *Big Fish Book*.

Jean Grolier de Servières, vicomte d'Aguisy (1479–1565), was government treasurer to François I of France. He had a collection of more than 3,000 books.

The statue of the river god Nile seated on a hippopotamus is now in the Vatican Museum, Rome. Coenen's source here, as so often, is Pierre Belon.

Left: Godlessness must be overcome and eradicated.
The bird (enemy of all snakes) is here depicted on a sceptre standing on the back of the hippopotamus. This means that the sceptre of justice violently overcomes and defeats the proud and godless.

Right: Sea horse. The fabulous horse of Neptune.
I have written more about this in my *Big Fish Book*. Adriaen Coenen van Schilperoort. 1585.

Sea swine

King Louis XII of France as archduke of Orléans and count of Blois had as his device a pig with sharp quills, like a hedgehog. The city of Blois traditionally combined that animal with the wolf in its device, and it can be found all over the place there carved in stone in the gates. There is also the house of a nobleman in this city with a pig carved in stone in the front wall, with two verses below:

Spicula sunt humili pax, sed bella superbo;
Et salus ex nostro vulnere, nexque venit.

Histrix is like a small pig with big long quills. They are common in Ethiopia. These creatures live near the water and also in caves and near rocks. It is strong on land and in the water. They are called iron swine. If they are angry or pursued, they loosen the bristles on their back and shoot them and wound people and dogs that approach them. As Rudolph writes in his commentary on the book of Leviticus, the *ciroqullus* is a creature with bristles and sharp quills just like the hedgehog or *hericius*, which is precisely a small pig full of sharp spines.

Coenen's text and image on the porcupine are taken from a work on heraldry: Claude Paradin, *Devises heroïques*, first published in Lyon in 1557. It was published in both French and Dutch (as *Princelijcke Deuisen*) in Antwerp in 1562–3. An English translation of the same work was published in London in 1591. The Latin text means: 'My quills spell peace to the humble but war to the proud / My wound brings health to the one, but destruction to the other.'

The text on the sea swine in the centre of the page virtually repeats that in Book 1. Radulfus Flaviacensis wrote a commentary on the Old Testament book of Leviticus. Coenen refers elsewhere to the description of the porcupine by St Isidore of Seville (c. 560–636), a Spanish ecclesiastic who wrote a voluminous encyclopaedia called *Etymologies or Origins*.

It is thought that the porcupine (*Hystrix cristata*) was introduced into Europe from Africa by the Romans. It was imported to England as a curiosity, and in the twelfth century William of Montpellier sent one to Henry II, who kept it in his park at Woodstock, Oxfordshire. Nowadays it is found in Italy and in parts of Greece.

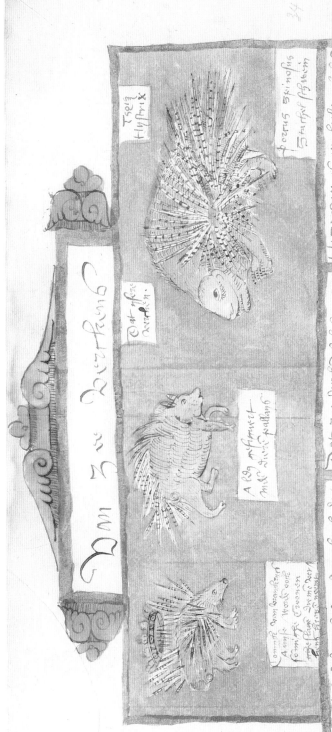

Vam Zee Veerkens

Tseer
Hystrix

porcus spinosus
Stachel Schwein

HISTRIX is een Beest is van...

SPICVLA SVNT SIMILI... SED
BELLA SVPERBO · ET SALVS EX
NOSTRO VVLNERE NEXT VENIT·

Sea lions

Left: In the time of Pope Martin IV, a fish with a lion's head was caught in the sea, and when it was brought on land it produced a terrible noise. It was taken to Rome and shown to everyone, after which great trouble followed.

Centre: The sea lion is like the land lion, but the latter roars and is more dangerous. The sea lion is tame in the water.

Right: A fish looking like this was said to have been caught before the death of Pope Paul III. A similar fish is also said to have been caught in the year 1284, to have cried like a human being, and to have been taken as a wonder to Pope Martin IV.

Martin IV was elected pope in 1281. Pope Paul III died in 1549.

The sea lion on the right goes back to the type depicted by Guillaume Rondelet in his *Libri de piscibus marinis* of 1554, where he refers to a certain Gisbertus Germanus in Rome for confirmation of its existence. Though Rondelet makes use of the illustration, he complains that artistic licence has led to a portrait that is not accurate.

Sea lions owe their name to the similarity to male lions of their thick manes and roaring. Sea lions and fur seals together form the family *Otariidae*. In contrast to seals, they have external ears and a pointed nose. They can raise themselves on their front flippers. Sea lions form dense and extremely noisy rookeries.

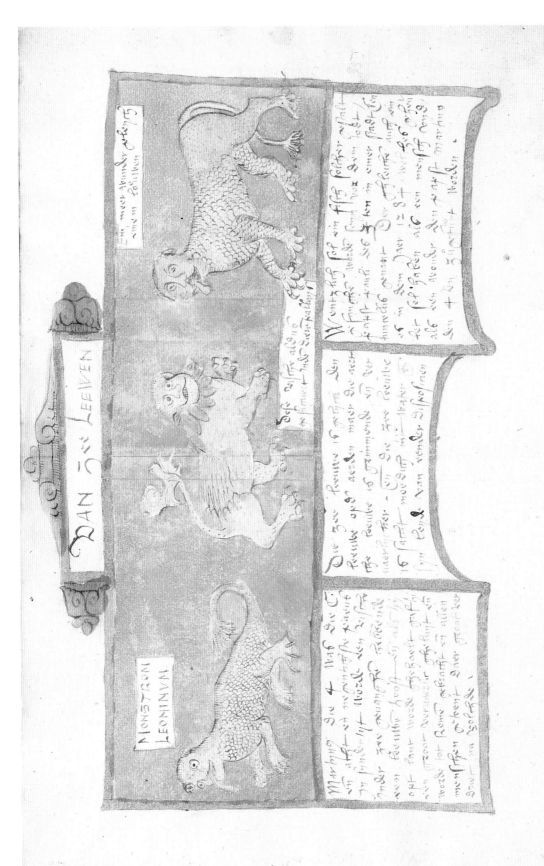

Sea monkeys

Aelian provides a thorough description of a sort of fish in the Red Sea that he calls sea monkey. It stretches its fins out like a flying fish. Behind the fin on its back it has a sharp protuberance that points backwards. His body is green with more brown on the back and a paler colour on the sides. The fish shown here came from the region of Dama.

This animal was found in Milan on a pile of stones and sent to Dr Gessner without further comment by the very learned scholar Hieronymus Cardano. The shape of the tail, however, makes it clear that it is an aquatic animal, although its head, fingers and feet do somewhat recall a monkey.

Aelian describes the sea monkey in *On Animals*, XII.27.

Girolamo Cardano (1501–1576) was a prolific natural scientist who worked for Pope Gregory XII in Rome from 1571 until his death.

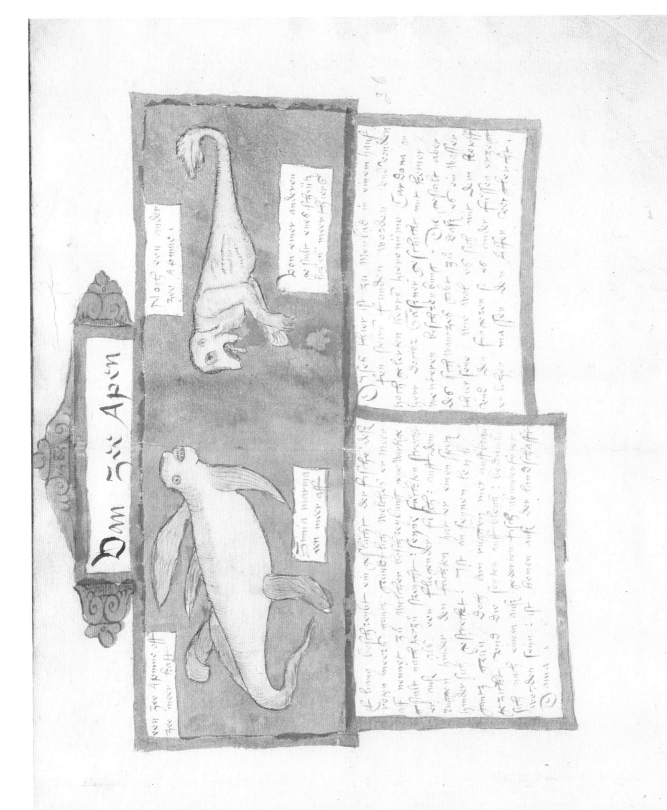

Sea wolves

Lupus marinus is the sea wolf. He resembles the land wolf because his greediness drives him to pursue the other fish in the water. When he is surrounded by nets, he digs a hollow in the sand with his tail, hides in it, and lets the nets pass over him. If he is caught on the hook, he is so agitated and wounds himself so much that he finally gets off the hook. The sea wolf bears young twice a year. In a harsh winter sea wolves are blind; that is when many blind sea wolves are caught.

This sea wolf is known to our Scheveningen fishermen and is also caught by the fishers who catch cod for salting (once it has been filleted and salted in a barrel, cod is called *aberdaan*). If these fishermen catch a sea wolf they salt it too, including the head and bones, and give the salted sea wolf as a present to good friends. It is also a tasty fish, better than the *aberdaan*. This sea wolf has a black belly, is white near the mouth full of a double row of strong teeth, and with a skin almost as slippery as an eel. I think it tastes better slightly salted than fresh. Fresh he tastes about as good as the *snottolf* or *kruikvis*, which also tastes better when slightly salted. Fresh he tastes a bit too much like a jellyfish.

The fish shown on the upper right is an accurate depiction of a wolf-fish (*Anarhichas lupus*) with the characteristic diagonal markings on its body. The wolf-fish can grow up to 1.25 metres in length. It has long teeth and very strong jaws, which give it such an awesome appearance. It is still regarded as a delicacy today.

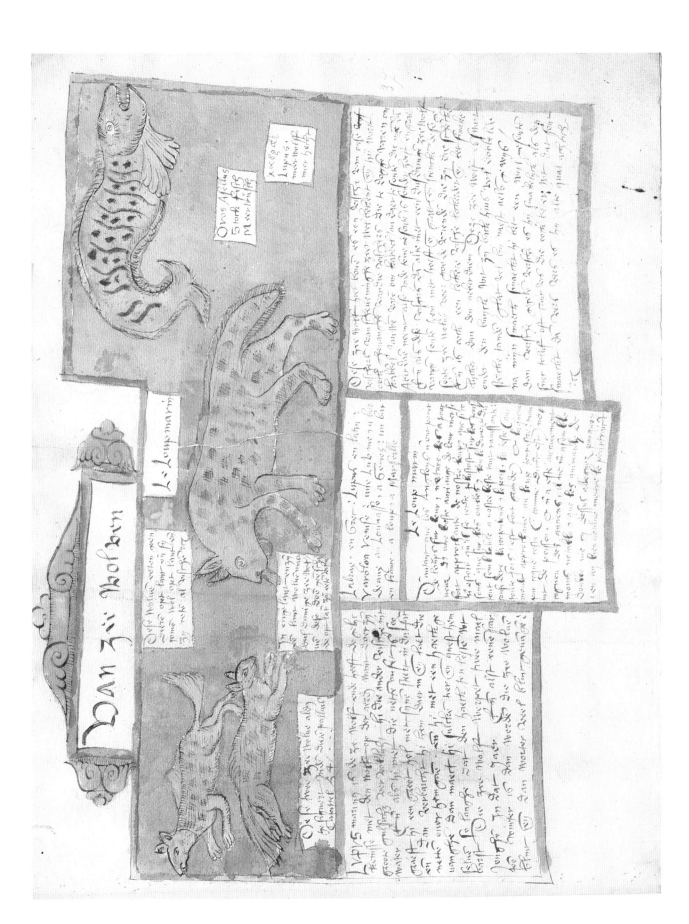

These three animals live both in the water and on land

The beaver is an animal like a dog. He has very sharp teeth and a beautiful coat, the blacker the more precious. His tail and back feet are regarded as fish, which is why the Roman Catholics are allowed to eat them on Fridays.

An otter. Otter flesh should not be eaten because it smells, but it is eaten in Germany. The Carthusian monks eat it, who are not allowed to eat most types of meat.

The sea dog or seal is also known as the *rob*. They are sometimes caught in the nets along the coast of Holland, but there are more of them on Vlieland, Tessel and the other islands. They have a sharp bite. Their back feet are lame; they use them for swimming. They walk with their front feet.

The images of the otter and seal – but not the beaver – are taken from Pierre Belon. As so often, Coenen compiles his composite pictures from different sources.

After becoming extinct in 1824, the European beaver was reintroduced in the Netherlands in 1990; since then it has been expanding slowly. The last wild otter was hit by a car in 1988. A reintroduction programme early in the twenty-first century has not yet been successful.

Two seal species occur in the North Sea: the harbour seal and the grey seal. A viral epidemic decimated the seals in 1988, but since then they have recovered to a healthy population level. Other seal species are stragglers from northern waters.

Strange sea hares

The sea hare is poisonous to humans and, vice versa, among the Indians humans are poisonous to the sea hare, for if he is just touched by a finger he dies, as Pliny states.
I have written more about these three types of sea hare in my *Big Fish Book*.

The sea hare is classified among the marine
gastropods, a class of molluscs. Sea hares are
nudibranches with often spectacular colours,
especially the ones that inhabit coral reefs.
At least six types of nudibranch inhabit the
southern waters of the North Sea. They are
usually small (between 5 and 12 centimetres),
but they are voracious predators.

Sepia or sea cat

When the hungry fisher is after me
I fool him by expelling blood.
It hides me as away I slip –
Let him rue it as he would –
Leaving blackness for every ship.
Like one who leads a simple life,
With yes to joy and no to toil,
Until the stern call he hears
Whose soul is fixed in this vale of tears.

The Lord God hates an untimely end,
So do your best to stay alive.
Your life does come from heaven sent,
To preserve it you must strive.
The sepia's tricks are his salvation,
He plies his wits and changes hue.
So you, blessed with a higher station,
Resourceful be in all you do.

A true account of what happened to me, Adriaen Coenen, in connection with these sea cats; an example that seems to be worthy of being included here.

It took place before the troubles in Holland, that is, before the iconoclasm and before there was any talk of Beggars and Papists. I was busy at the time making a big fish book in which I collected all the fish, worms, serpents and suchlike that I could find, on the basis of what I saw at sea every day, heard from the fishermen and learned from questioning them, as well as what I found in fish books that had been made before my time. While I was working on that, Milord Cornelis Suys, Lord of Rijswijk and President of Holland at the time, also lent me a fish book in which I found material for my book. That fish book was also a big book, made by a doctor called Rondelet.

Since Milord the president had great pleasure in the big fish book that I made and it was often in his house when he had visitors, I was regularly invited to dine with him. Thus it happened that I passed by his house on the way to Scheveningen – where I lived at the time – and he was at the window and said: 'Adri, come and dine with me tomorrow. I shall show you fish which I don't think are in your book' I replied: 'Yes, Milord, that's quite possible. I can hardly know everything.' The next day I was his guest, very curious to know what kind of fish these would be, and when I sat there in the afternoon at table with him and various other gentlemen and the meal was almost over, Milord the president said to his page: 'Go to the room and bring me that bundle of fish.' I wondered what kind of fish they might be. The page came back with a bundle with six dried sea cats. Then Milord the president asked me:

'Adri, what kind of fish are those?' I replied: 'Milord, they are dried sepia in Latin, although I'm not a Latinist.' Well', said Milord, 'how do you know them? I have been told that they are not to be found on the fish market here in The Hague.' At which I said: 'Yes, sir, our fishers in Scheveningen throw them away when they catch them with the other fish. They consider them to be poor fish.' Milord the president thought that this could not be true, and asked: 'Why do they throw them away?' I said: 'We do not consider them edible, and our fishers call them sea cats. And cats aren't edible.'

Then Milord began to laugh loudly at what I had said about the sea cats. Milord said that he had been tormented enough when he had to eat sea cats when he was at school in Orléans in France. If he went to the kitchen on a fish day and asked the girls what they were preparing, it was always sepia. 'And I wondered,' he said, 'why I never saw them here. Adri, would you get a pair for me if you can get them from the fishers, and I will reward whoever brings them?' 'Yes, sir, if I am alive and well I shall bring them for you tomorrow.' And I did too, because it was summer and then our fishers catch them together with the other fish. I often sent him them. He rewarded those who brought the fish with food and money. Milord the president and Milord of Oosterwijk enjoyed it very much and found it a delicate dish, as they told me. Milord the president also told me that the bundle of sepias had been sent from Rouen, and that a bundle of six sepias had also been sent to the stadholder of Holland, the Prince of Orange, as a great delicacy and special dish. I had to have them sent regularly to Milord of Oosterwijk from Scheveningen. This is what I have described here and it is a true happening. Do not be unduly surprised by it.

Three sorts of sea cats

We call the left-hand one a Spanish sea cat.
We call the middle one a sea cat.
Our fishers call the right-hand one a sea spider, and some who have investigated the matter a bit call it *poelomp*.

The common squid (*Loligo vulgaris*) on the left has a torpedo-shaped body that can grow to 50 centimetres. It has a siphon through which it can pump a strong current of water. This enables it to race away at top speed when in danger. Like the sepia, the common squid moves to shallow waters in May or June to breed and lay eggs. The eggs are strung in long white bunches from pieces of wood, rocks and other objects.

The sepia (*Sepia officinalis*) in the middle is a cephalopod that can grow up to 30 centimetres. It is broad and flat in shape, with ten short arms at the front of the head. It lives in shallow waters in May and August, spending the winter in deeper water. It blackens its eggs with ink and attaches them to seaweed or other slender objects.

The octopus (*Octopus vulgaris*) on the right is the classic octopus. It occurs world-wide to a depth of 200 metres. Today the octopus is over-exploited in many regions.

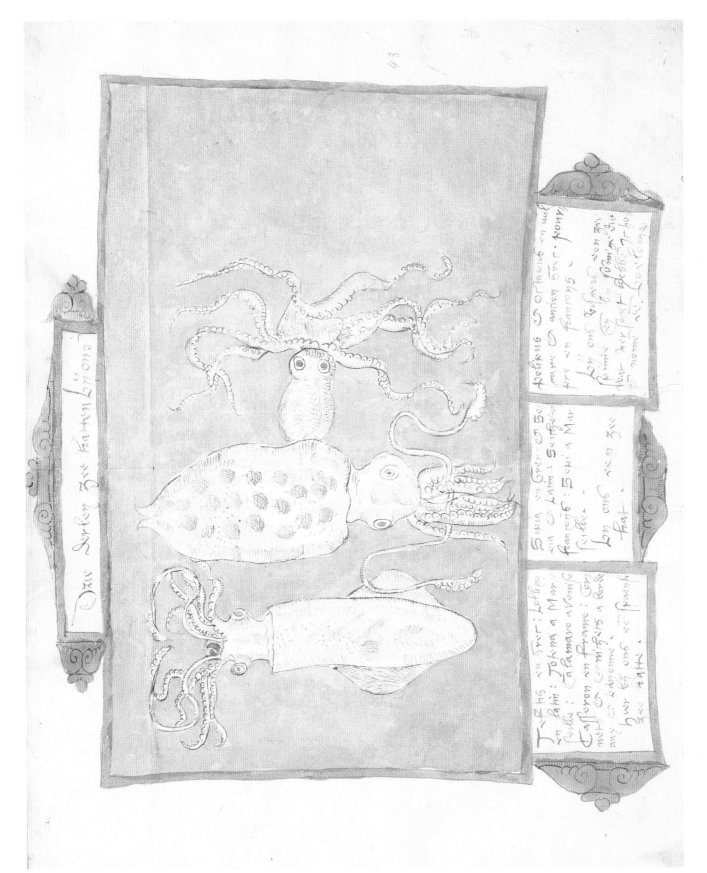

The fish illustrated here is shown in many places for money

This fish is called a Spanish sea cat by the fishermen of Scheveningen. Its body is 2 feet 2 thumbs long and 1.5 feet wide. On 15 November 1566 I, Adriaen Coenen, bought such a fish from a seaman in Scheveningen called Cornelis Senten, who had caught it while fishing for shrimps close to the shore. Another fish like this was found that same year on 17 November between Scheveningen and Katwijk. This one was shown all over the country for payment, and this image of it appeared in print.

This big lobster seizes swimmers. The monster Rhinocer in turn eats up the large 12-foot lobster

This wondrous sea monster called Rhinocer is said to eat up the large sea crab (shown here), which is twelve feet long. This picture of the large sea crab was made in Venice. It looks different from the common sea crab, larger and with a different colour: he is dark brown with many patches of white, red and blue. When boiled or roasted he turns red, like all crustaceans. This large lobster can drag a swimmer down to the sea bed with its claws. This is plausible, even if it applied to our ordinary lobsters.

The Atlantic lobster (*Homarus gammarus*) is a large, bluish-black lobster that forages on the sea bed at night. Normally lobsters that are fished are not bigger than 45 centimetres, but the largest ever caught (in England in 1931) measured 1.25 metres. The lobster does not travel very far. It has a narrow, armoured body. The front two legs are long with big claws, the others are for crawling over the sea bed. Lobsters can also swim backwards very fast.

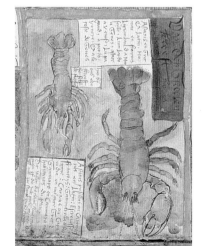

165

A *poelomp*

On Monday 11 October 1546 I who write this, Adriaen Coenen, bought this fish at the Scheveningen auction. The auctioneer was Ysbrant Michiels, former sheriff of Scheveningen. This fish was caught by fishermen from Krimpen, who had caught it in their nets. I took this fish and my other fish to my home in The Hague and summoned a painter to portray it. Soon afterwards I sold it to two adventurers for 7 Carolus guilders. They put it on show for payment and travelled with it to all kinds of towns. It was a strange-looking fish, which is seldom seen by our fishers. The two fins on either side of the head looked a bit like the wings of a bat. Later I had another one, but it didn't have wings like these. This fish sticks so tightly to something – a boat or a fish – with the round pads on its tails that it is almost impossible to remove it, at least if it is still alive. That is why it is called the fish with the thousand mouths. This fish had a curved beak, black and hard like that of a parrot or hawk, and eyes as big as those of a cow. He was about 3 feet long, but including the tails if they protruded forwards it was 7 feet.

This was an unusually large animal for this part of the North Sea. Squid usually live in deep water. The largest species is the giant squid (*Architeutis dux*), which can be 18 metres long including the tentacles. They are occasionally found dead on the shore or in a net. By the nineteenth century the scars left by squids' suckers on the skins of sperm whales triggered the hypothesis that gigantic squids must exist.

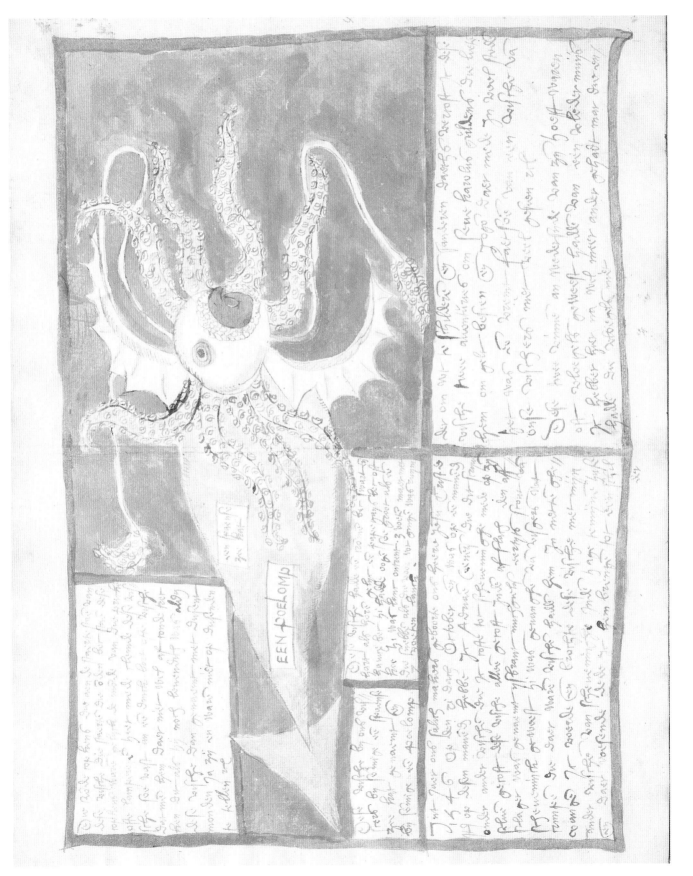

EEN POELOMP

Poelomp

I once had a fish like this, which had been caught by our fishers. I dried it as a curiosity. His body was like a round copper pot that could hold more than 4 pints, excluding the long tails that hang over its beak. Those tails are covered with innumerable little heads or pads, with which he seizes other fish and sticks to them. I've seen them on other occasions here as well, but they were smaller. They rarely come here. I've also found them in a cod that had swallowed them. They were not completely digested.

Aelian states that if the octopus is caught by the eagle and carried into the air, it tries to wreath its tentacles around the eagle's wings to throw the eagle off balance. If it manages to do so, it pulls the eagle down and drowns it in the water.

This octopus is a peril to shipwrecked mariners, because he sucks the blood out of their body, drags them below the surface and holds them there until they drown. Each pad on these tails sucks like the mouth of a lamprey. I who write this have looked into the matter.

Aelian describes the struggle between eagle and octopus in *On Animals*, VII.11.

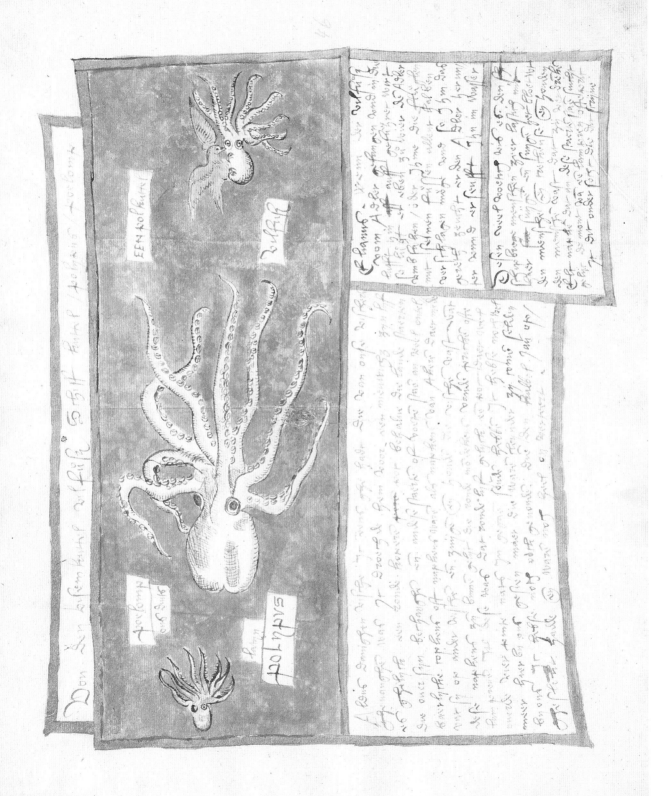

These are all *pijlstaarten*

Centre: This illustration of this eagle-fish was sent from Italy by the scholar Cornelius Sittardus to Professor Conrad Gessner.

Right: This is our *pijlstaart*, drawn from life.

Our fishermen on the coast of Holland are familiar with the *pijlstaart*. It is caught in the summer with other fish in the nets. This fish is not eaten here. Our fishers usually throw it away, but they keep the liver, from which they make oil that is good for broken or bruised limbs. Because nowadays all these fish fetch higher prices than in the past and everything is expensive, there are many poor fishermen who dry these *pijlstaarten* and eat them. The fishmongers take them to the fish markets now. They cut off the tail with the spear that sticks out of it, as you can see here, and sell these *pijlstaarten*. Those who don't know them suppose they are rays.

All three images derive from Pierre Belon. Coenen claimed to have dried thousands of rays in his youth to make dragon-like 'Jenny Hanivers' (see inset).

The depictions with the long tail and spine at the base of the tail are reasonably accurate for the common eagle ray (*Myliobatis aquila*) that is found in shallow waters off the coasts of Europe and West Africa. It is uncommon in the North Sea. It can achieve a span of more than 75 centimetres and a length of 1.5 metres. About 40 types of eagle ray have been identified all over the world. The largest and best-known is the giant manta ray, which can achieve a span of 6 metres.

AQVILA MARINA

These are fish called *torpedo, krampvis*

Left: On 12 July 1582 a fisherman in Scheveningen called Cornelis Cornelis alias Stump caught a torpedo like the one painted here, with the belly on one side and the back on the other. If you touch a torpedo while it is still alive, your limbs are paralysed. The fishermen who helped to catch this fish were all paralysed in their hands. It took three days for the paralysis to disappear in the case of one of them. This really happened. Others who have written about fish have also mentioned that he stuns people and other fish if they touch him. When he stuns fish, they cannot swim away and he eats them.

This illustration was sent by the scholar Cornelius Sittardus to Professor Conrad Gessner.

This is the common electric ray (*Torpedo nobiliana*), a close relative of the marbled electric ray presented by Coenen in Book 1. He has drawn both a spotted and a non-spotted form.

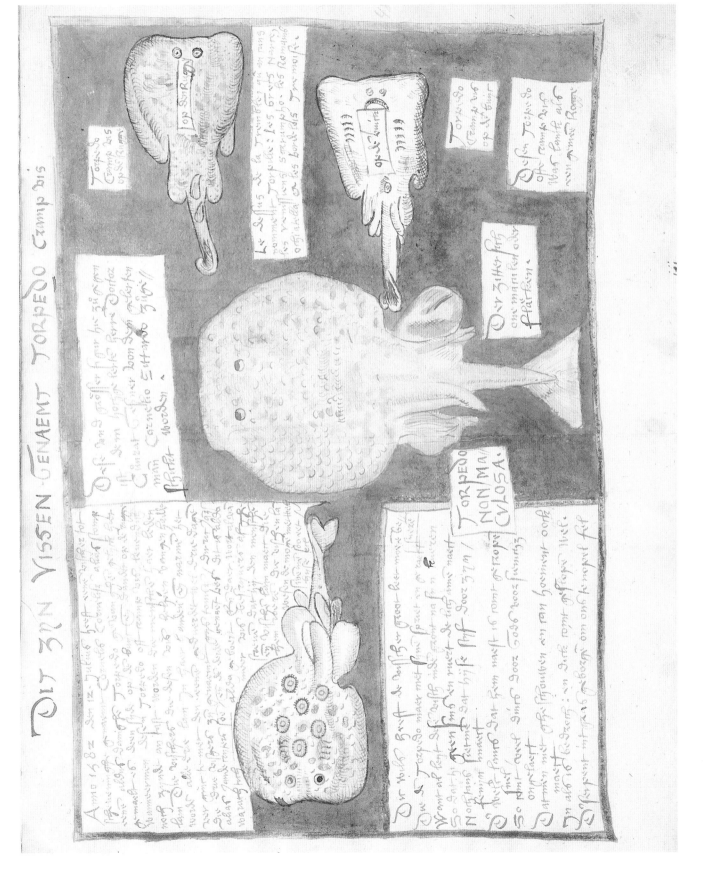

173

Urtica marina, sea nettles

In Holland they are called jellyfish. Pliny says in Book 9: *Urtica* is a fish that moves and hunts its food by night. Anyone who touches this fish is stung, just as nettles on land sting if you touch them. Aristotle says that the creature called the sea nettle is large and stings by itself. It has no hard shell on its body, but is like other creatures that have flesh. This creature steals and seizes all it can with its hands, and then sticks to the stone like an octopus. Its mouth is in the middle of its body. I have written more about jellyfish in my *Big Fish Book*. Our fishers also say that these jellyfish sting and bite the hands and eyes when they are picked up.

Many a fisher feels terrible pain
When the torpedo grazes him with its sting
For though this fish likes the bed of the main
And avoids touching a moving thing
He's quick to give a poisonous dose
To whatever creature comes too close.
God's providence offers many a thing
That passes beyond man's understanding,
Like deceit, which often comes to pass
Hiding like a serpent in the grass.

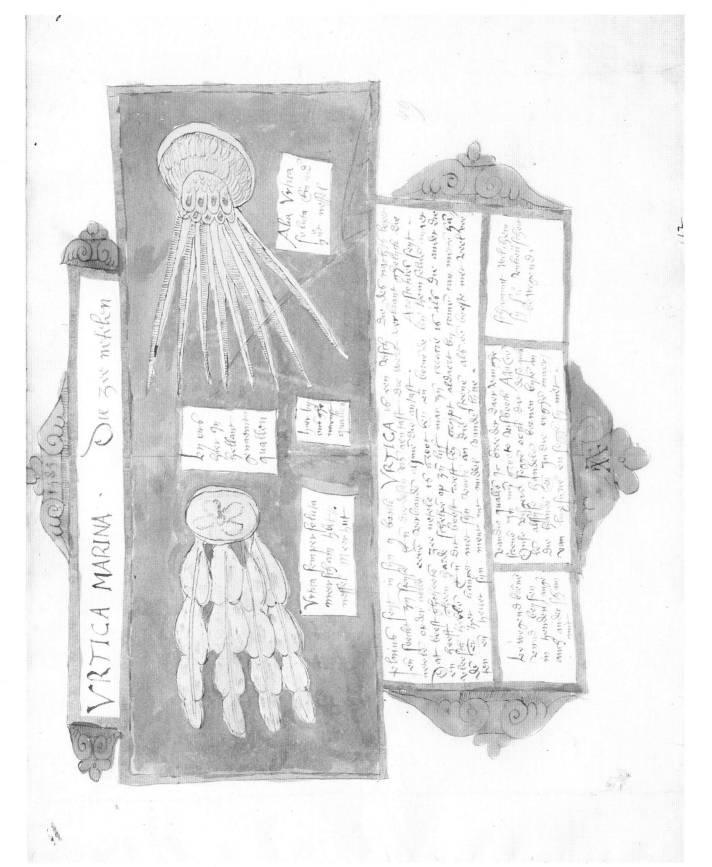

Other kinds of sea nettles

The German author writes: this is edible; he clings to the rocks in the sea so tightly that he can only be pulled off in pieces.

These small jellyfish or sea nettles are like walnuts, some red, others greenish or bluish, and some are dazzling white like crystal or diamonds. I have written more about them in my *Big Fish Book*, as well as about how they are sometimes washed up in large numbers on the shore in Holland.

The jellyfish on the right is the Lion's Mane. Jellyfish are coelenterates. They move by contracting their umbrella-like dome, but they are classified as animal plankton because they cannot swim against the tide. They are 98 per cent water. All jellyfish have stinging cells, but only a few are able to penetrate the human skin. Jellyfish live on phytoplankton.

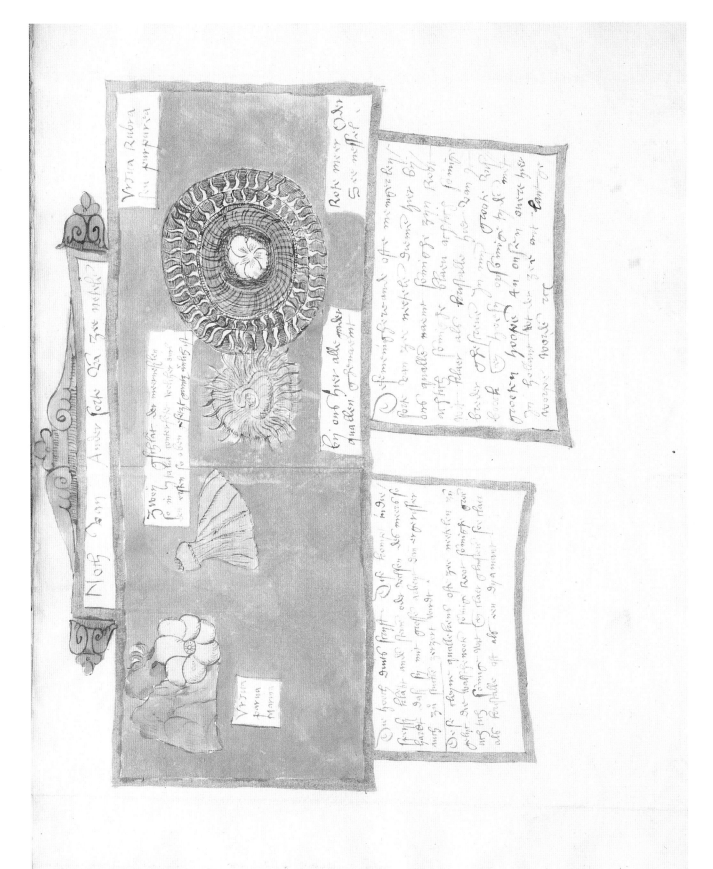

Round plants with rough and sharp spines on their shell, and another kind of plant that is as bald as an egg is the coot's egg

Left: These sea apples or sea urchins owe their name to their resemblance to the hedgehog, because their shell is completely covered with sharp spines. Three types are distinguished. The commonest type is the one in which eggs are found; the largest is the size of an egg. They have a lovely colour when they are alive – most are purple, some are brown, green or blue – but the colours disappear when they are dead. They can grow to quite a size in some places. They lose their spines when they are dead. It is a very wondrous and rare creature of the sea. There are also many as small as walnuts. Our fishers know them; they catch them in the nets in which they catch flounder and plaice. They are not eaten here. I cannot see anything in them except a few intestines and they were full of sand. So I can't imagine that they are edible. I have often found them on the shore.

Right: The coot's egg has a very thin shell and is fragile. They occasionally wash up on our coast and are cast ashore in large quantities when there is a heavy storm. They usually look like the one shown here with a hole in the middle. They are generally empty, or contain nothing but sand. That is why I and others think that they are the eggs of some animal, or plants of the sea. O, what wonders are wrought in the sea by God almighty. May he be praised. Amen.

This one is heart-shaped, less round than the last, and only has a few small spines. The inside looks very different too. We often find them on the shore, but always as empty as an empty eggshell. I have never heard of our fishers finding a full one. O good and wonderful God, how wonderful you are in all your works. May you be praised for ever. Amen.

Sea urchins, including the edible *Echinus esculentus*, consist of a hollow shell filled with internal organs and eggs or sperm. Their skin (actually an exoskeleton) is a shell made of calcium slivers. Their feet poke out through openings in the shell. Sea urchins filter sediment as they eat. They usually hide under rocks in the daytime and go in search of food at night.

Coenen's coot's eggs are the egg-shaped skeletons of sea urchins that have been washed up.

When eaten raw, they are considered a delicacy in some countries.

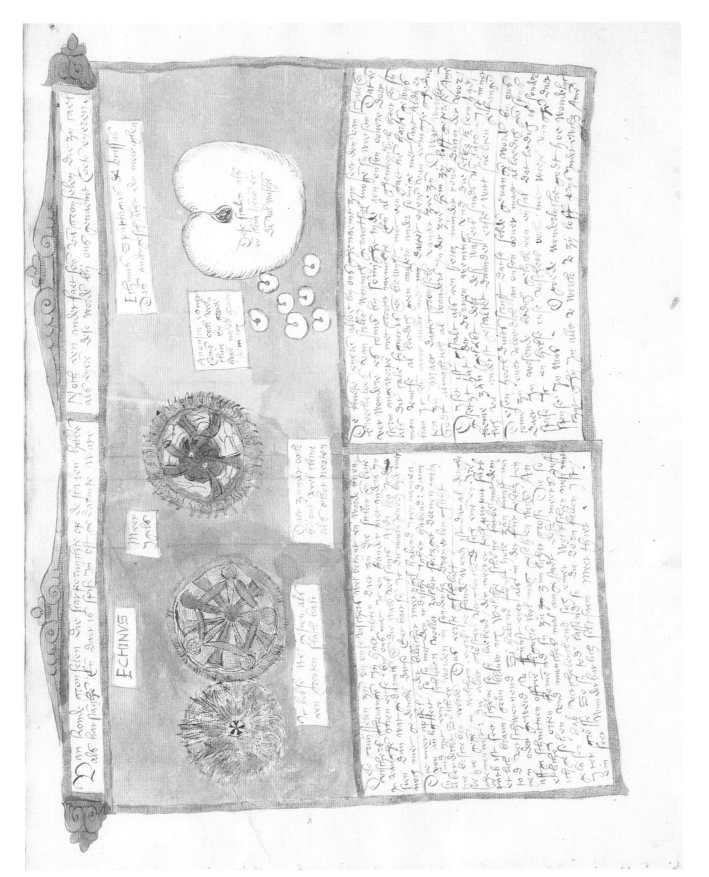

Zoophytes

The sea cucumber is just like the land cucumber in shape, colour and taste.

The sea clove. This plant looks very different from the clove flower from which its name is derived. It is covered by a red skin, and if it is peeled, a substance full of holes appears, like a sieve. It grows on stones and on wood that has been in the water for a long time. It grows from beneath from a shell as though it comes from a root.

Epipetrum. This is six fingers long, one and a half fingers wide, partly black and partly red.

Malum insanum marinum. This plant closely resembles a fruit called mad-apple. *Uva marina*. This is a kind of fungus that hangs from a shell and has flowers on the outside.

The mad-apple is the aubergine (compare Italian *melanzana*).

Sea cucumbers (*Holothuroidea*) form a widespread group of creatures, usually with a soft skin. They are found in great diversity on the ocean bottom at all depths, especially in coral reefs. The smallest are 1 centimetre long, while the giant sea cucumber (*Synapta maculata*) can grow to 5 metres. In cold waters many sea cucumbers find shelter in deep-water coral (*Lophelia pertusa*). Reefs of this coral are considered to be the rainforests of the North Atlantic. The largest such reefs in British waters, the Darwin hills, were discovered west of Scotland in 1997.

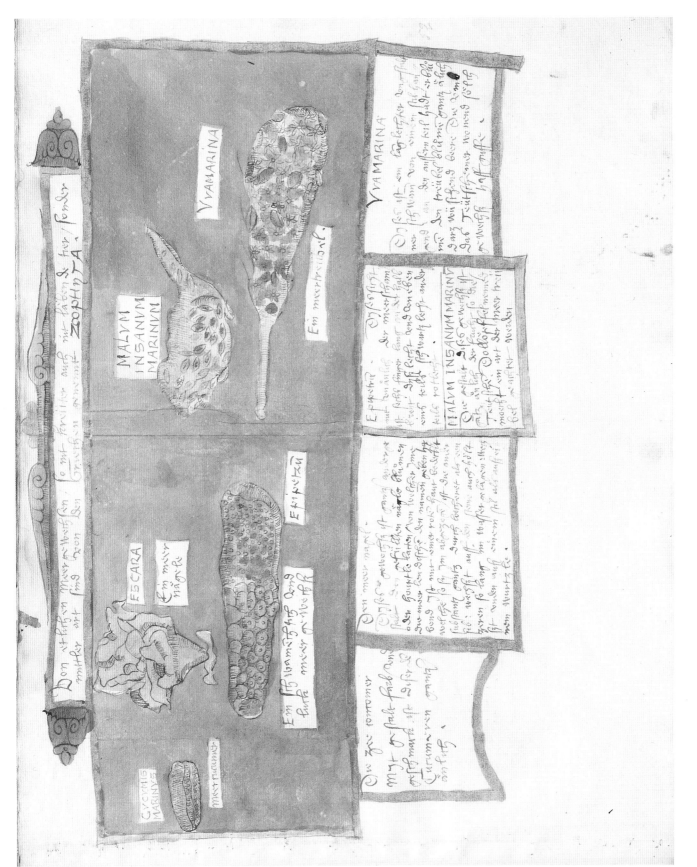

Seaworms and other strange plants that grow on rocks and cliffs in the sea

Lower left: Our fishermen call these *strandveertjes* and catch them in their herring nets. The fishers set them on their caps, and when the feathers are dry, they put them back in the water and they bud like the rose of Jericho.

Centre: I have written a lot of curious details about these seaworms and plants that grow on stones in the sea and on rocks on the coast that are washed by the sea in my *Big Book*. Here I merely show you their shapes and names.

Lower right: These fingers and thumbs, as our fishers call them, cannot be distinguished from real human hands, except by their colour and because they are swollen because of the water in them. Our fishers catch them on hooks near rocky sea beds.

182

Sea grapes, sponges and the dill that grows on rocks in the sea in Scotland

I don't know what kind of plants these grapes are. I have found them attached to oysters, and usually their berries are dry and empty. They come floating in like grape skins and are stuck to one another. I have found them the size of two human heads, one head or smaller. They are whitish, pale and sometimes a bit reddish. I have also found some that contained something liquid in the berries; the content was a bit reddish like in a rotten egg where the yolk and white are mixed. That is why I and many others suspect that it is the roe that some fish or other has emitted and which has not been able to develop. That is why it is dried and washes up on the coast of Holland.

There are many sponges on the Norwegian coast. Sponges have life in them. Injustice is hard for everyone to bear. 1585.

If the watery sponge is gently prised
With care from the stony rock
It trembles to feel such a shock.
So painfully are people surprised
By the violence they see on all sides.
Of hatred and envy they take stock
And towards vengeance swiftly slide.
'Tis seen as foolish to be pliable,
But as the sponge the water does imbibe,

So patience — 'tis undeniable —
Suffers injustice. But when brought to view,
The judge will punish injustice as due,
And reward patience with verdicts true.
Sweet will be the recompense of the just,
While the wicked punishments await.
So do good works, in God your trust,
For that will foster love and end hate.

Dill is a leaf or herb that grows on the cliffs of the Scottish and English coast, as our fishers say who fish for herring there off the coast. When heavy storms blow, large quantities of this dill end up on the coast of Holland. Yes, sometimes you could fill a hundred carts with the dill stretching a mile along the coast. I have often found this dill with pieces of stone or chalk in it. When I was young we children played with it and called it *kermes* because it consisted of such a strange plant. We made whistles, key-rings and belts from these round things, because this plant is as tough as leather. It hardly rots, but is hardened by the sun and sand. As our fishers say, it spreads far out to sea from the rocks. This dill has cost the life of many a shipwrecked mariner, because it is impossible to swim through it to land. The swimmer gets tangled up in it. Our fishers say that children in Scotland eat this dill, but that is hard to believe, even though every country has its own customs and unusual tastes.

The 'dill' referred to here is a type of seaweed like bladderwrack. Kermes is the name given to the dried bodies of adult females of the scale insect (*kermes ilicis*) which form hard berry-like galls on the kermes oak. They were used to make vermilion dye and medicine.

Sponges (*Porifera*) are mainly stationary marine creatures with (in most cases) a regular shape. They have a very simple calcium skeleton or a network of spongine, a silk-like material. Sponges have no mouth, digestive system or organs, nor do they have a perceptible nerve system. In fact, they are nothing but filters. The water enters through small openings in the surface. Inside the body of the sponge a sort of vacuum is created, enabling the sponge to pump more than four times its own volume per minute through its body and to filter microscopic organisms. The filtered water leaves the body through a larger exit hole.

Salt and freshwater worms

What the Germans write about the sea louse. This animal is covered with a thin shell, the size and width of a bean, and is a terrible plague to fish. It sticks to them and does not let go until it has sucked the fish completely dry.

What they write about the sea flea. This is another plague to the fish, it has a thin shell as well, and is so small that it takes a lot of effort to spot it.

Worms are found here in the ditches. They stick to the legs of people who go barefoot into the ditch. If they have stuck to a leg, it is best to wait until they drop off again. If you pull them off, the spot where they have attached themselves becomes infected, but that does not happen if they fall off themselves. If you pull them off, they leave part of their teeth in your skin.

Tadpoles come from frogs. From the eggs that frogs and toads lay in water come tadpoles, until they lose their tails and become frogs. I have found this out myself.

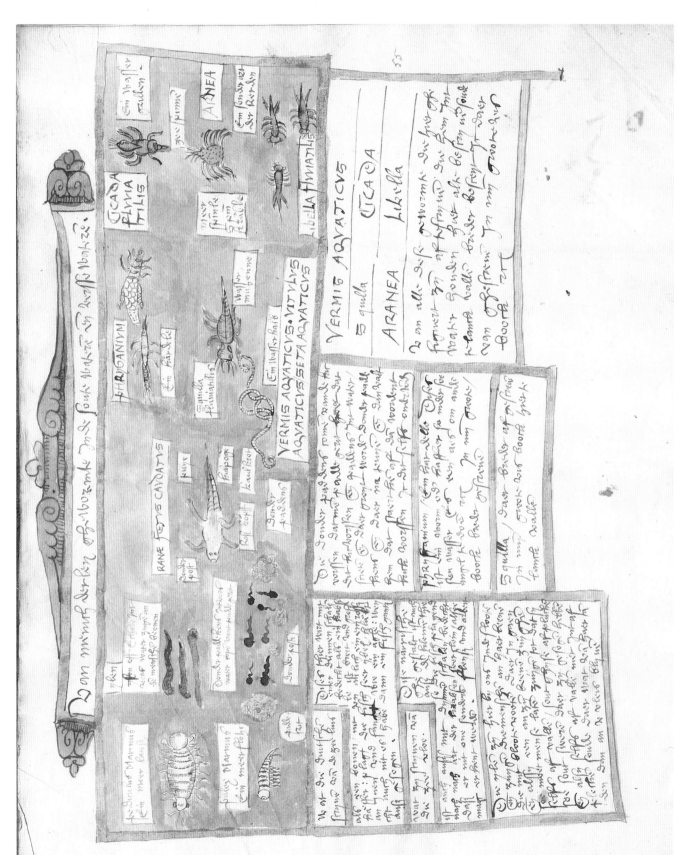

Round and long flabs that are not jellyfish

These round flabs, as our fishermen call them, are said to cling to the rocky sea bed. If there is a heavy storm and the sea is very wild, they are torn loose and wash up on the shore in large numbers. Large quantities of shellfish are caught using these flabs as bait – more than with any other bait. If there has been one of those storms that wash up these flabs, many of us go to the shore and women and children collect them.

These long flabs are also washed up on our coast when there has been a storm at sea. Our fishers use them as bait to catch cod, but since it is such a flaccid substance, they do not like using it and prefer a different bait, even though it is free.

To buy what costs nothing, isn't that sad?
But our fishers have found an answer to that.

Bottom right: Our fishers call this a sea mouse. It is a strange sort of seaworm. Our fishers catch them in the flounder nets. These sea mice have all kinds of colours and are hairy; they may be poisonous. They lose their colours when they are dead. It is a strange worm that is usually caught when the weather is warm.

The sea mouse (*Aphrodite aculeata*) is a strange-looking worm. It is really a coelenterate, can reach a length of 20 centimetres, and is twice as long as it is wide. Its back is covered with felt-like mouse-grey hairs, bordered with tough spines, which have fantastic iridescent colours. Sea mice live half buried in sand and eat all kinds of creatures of the sea bed.

The familiar seaworms are bristleworms. Nowadays two species are distinguished: the lugworm (*Arenicola marina*) and the black lugworm (*A. defodiens*). They bury in the sand, but betray their whereabouts by the presence of worm-casts. They have been used as bait for centuries.

Worms called suckers, a strange seaworm, rare seaworms

Left: Our fishers in Scheveningen call these worms suckers. They attach themselves to fish like lampreys. When they attach themselves to cod, they are caught with the cod and hauled aboard. I've been sent them by fishers on the herring boats. The longest are as long as a large human foot and as thick as a man's finger. They are pale red when alive and black when they are dried, I was told. They are ugly, inedible worms. The lampreys also fasten themselves to fish, but they are edible and tasty. In fact, they are considered to have a delicate flavour and are rated very highly.

Centre: Sea horse. I was given a worm like this; it was dried by a man from Utrecht who bought rare dried fish from me. This creature is not familiar here.

Right: Ondochten or *stoppelruen.* The topmost of these seaworms or small fish has a narrow, finless tail like a worm; the other has a tail like a fish. They occur in both varieties. These worms or fish are caught by our Scheveningen fishers in the flounder nets when the summer starts to get warm. They are inedible, have a tough skin and hardly any meat. They are worm-like, some smooth, others with a tougher, scaly skin like the sturgeon. I have written more about them in my *Big Fish Book.*

The images of the seahorse in the centre and the seaworm on the lower right are both taken from Belon.

These small fish belong to the viviparous family of seahorses and pipefishes, of which the small seahorse (*Hippocampus ramulosus*) occurs in the Netherlands. There are many beautifully coloured seahorses. The smallest of the 35 types that have been described is only 4 centimetres long, while the largest, the giant seahorse, can reach a length of 30 centimetres. Between 50 and 1,500 babies spend two or three weeks in the pouch of the male.

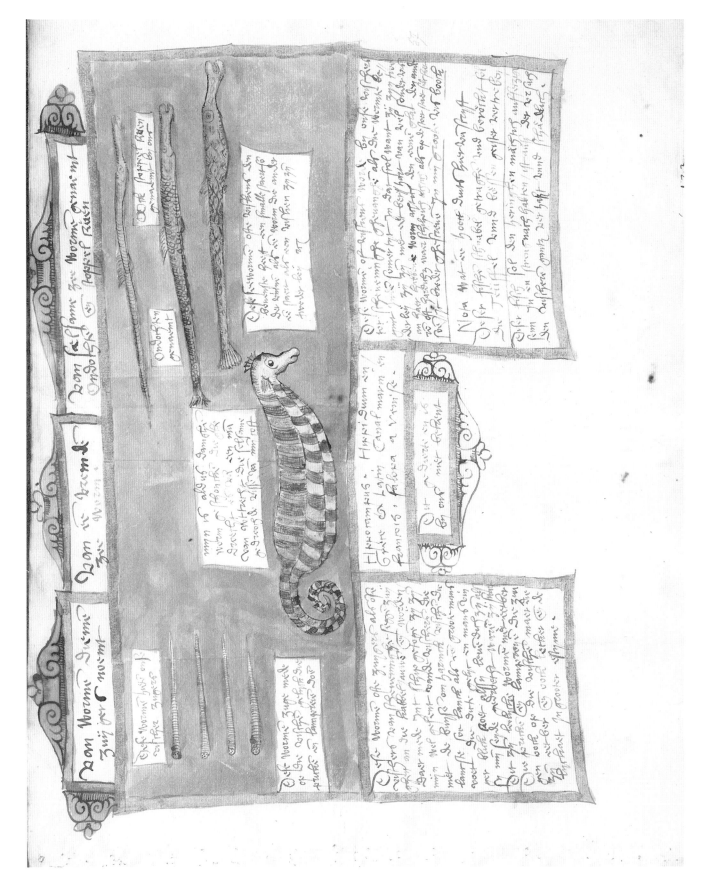

All kinds of starfish called five-footers

We have starfish of all kinds, as you can see in this illustration. The small ones are found in the fish that feed on them; the large ones get stuck to the baited hooks and the fishermen say that the fish won't bite because the starfish are sucking off the bait. 1585.

The common starfish (*Asteria rubens*) is widespread in coastal waters from the flood-line to a depth of about 200 metres. More than 1,600 types have been identified. The extraordinary feature of starfish is that they change from a bilateral symmetry as a larva to a radial symmetry as an adult. Starfish are able to regenerate large parts of their body if they are mutilated. They can also reverse their stomach to digest a prey externally. This enables them to squeeze their stomach into a mussel-shell. Their diet consists mainly of bivalves (mussels), but they will occasionally eat a dead crab.

Common starfish, rare starfish

Left: Our common starfish. They are usually reddish in colour. An old saying runs: 'The starfish never did anyone any good, except a man who won a sheep's cheese with one.'

Centre: Stella arborensis. This starfish is rarely caught. It is kept with care as an unusual spectacle and marine wonder.

Right: A starfish with 13 tails. A fisherman from Scheveningen called Maarten Vrancken, who had been fishing for herring, once gave me a starfish with thirteen tails. He had caught it far out at sea; it was a reddish purple, and pale. Our common starfish are usually a reddish brown and not purple, like hands. This starfish with 13 tails was the size of the biggest common starfish. O God, how wonderful you are in all your works. May you be praised for ever more.

Starfish are found with 5, 13, 15, 22 or 27 arms. Coenen's thirteen-arm starfish may have been a sunstar, a starfish that can grow to a diameter of 35 centimetres and have between eight and fourteen arms. It is fairly rare in the south of the North Sea, since it lives in more northerly waters.

Sea pigeons

Left: This fish is caught around the mouth of the Nile. It is as round as a bottle, without scales, and has a rough hard skin, with spines like a hedgehog. He has a small mouth with four teeth. He is not edible, because this fish consists of nothing but head and belly. Usually the skin is removed, filled with cotton, and sold in other countries. It is hung as a decoration in apothecaries' shops and other places.

Centre: Orbis. The skin of this fish is removed and filled with straw.

Right: This fish is round too, but has a long mouth. Some call it the sea cock, because when he is suspended, he turns to the wind with his mouth and thus indicates from which direction the wind is coming.

The image of the pufferfish is taken from Belon.

Coenen discusses the pufferfish (*Tetra-dontidae*) together with the equally spherical lumpsucker, which he also presents in Book 1. Pufferfish are found mainly in warmer waters; many live near coral reefs. They can inflate themselves enormously, and some, like the porcupine fish (*Diodontidae*), here shown on the bottom right, have tough prickles on their body. They are still dried, stuffed and exhibited today. A very well-known pufferfish is the poisonous Japanese fugu (*Fugu rubripes*), one of the deadliest delicacies in the world.

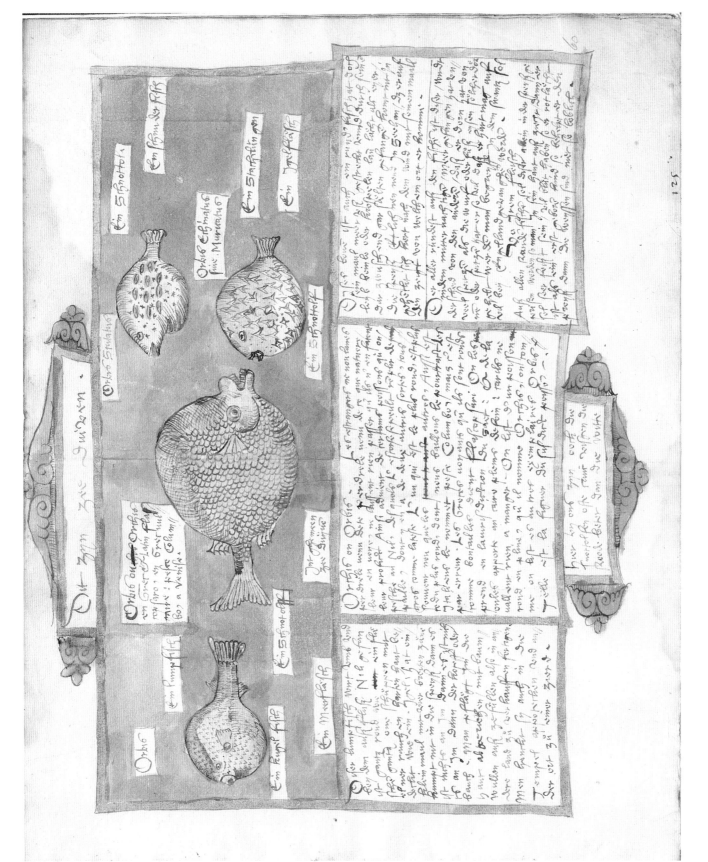

Three sorts of lumpsuckers or pitcher-fish

Left: This is a genuine pitcher-fish, caught by the English. His back is light red, his belly white. Apparently he has no bones and has a mouth like a frog, small eyes and a rough skin. A delicious fish to eat.

Centre: A fish is caught in the German sea like the one illustrated here, for this one was painted from life. Its back is roughly the colour of a frog on land, while the belly is bluish and green.

Right: This very terrible fish is caught in the Baltic. It has a thick skin with many spines.

Some 25 types of lumpsucker have been identified, which are all found in the cool waters of the northern hemisphere.

198

Three kinds of *hoosmonden* (sea devils)

Hoosmond is the word used by our fishermen in Scheveningen. It is an ugly fish with a very big mouth as wide as its belly. It has a very big belly with a fin on each side, as if they were the feet or claws of its belly. The tail tapers to a point. He has narrow, sharp teeth on the upper and lower jaws, and long, erect, pointed fins on his head and back. His skin is as thin as parchment, unlike the ray or sturgeon, and much thinner. His back is completely black, his belly white, and he is smooth all over. The biggest or longest I ever saw was 5 feet long. Our fishers catch them in the flounder nets. He is not edible. They throw him away. We and others dry the skin to stuff it for decoration.

The image is derived from Belon.

The anglerfish (*Lophius piscatorius*) can grow to a length of 2 metres, but is usually caught between 50 and 60 centimetres long. It has become an important fish for the commercial market. Its appearance is terrifying, with its gigantic head, long teeth, slimy skin and spines on its back. In many languages it is known as the sea devil.

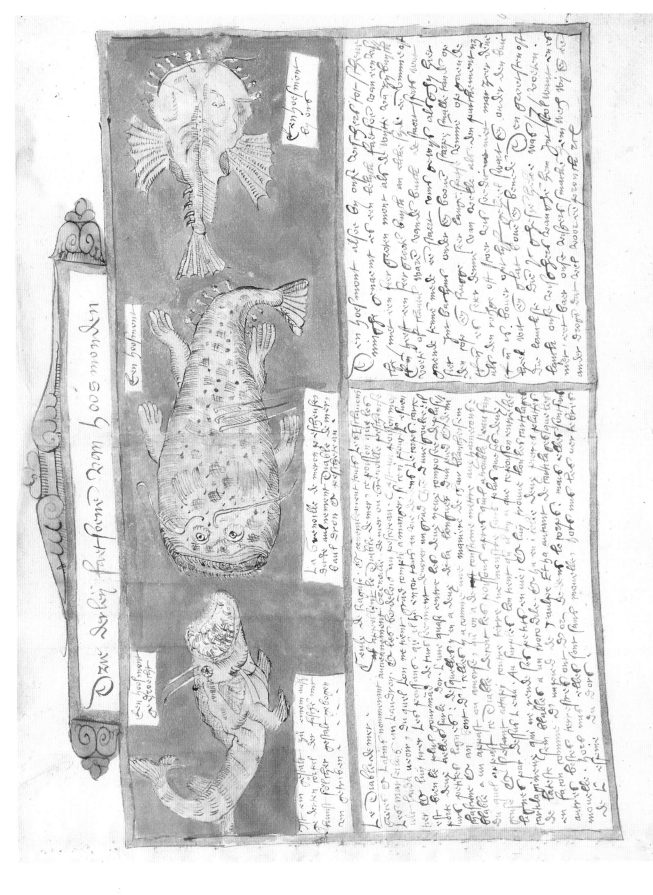

Four rare fish from newly discovered foreign lands

Coenen cites from French and German texts (not translated here) concerning four fish: Scolopax, Capriscus, Ostracion Nili and the Ostracion Americae or Tamoata. The latter is a variant of a Tupi word still in use in Brazil for the callichthyid armoured catfish, a freshwater species very common in north-east Brazil.

The fish on the upper right is a snipefish (*Macroramphosus scolopax*). This reddish fish lives on the sea bed and is about 20 centimetres long. It is also found in the North Sea.

The fish on the upper left may be the yellow boxfish (*Ostracion cubicus*), a genuine coral fish. The depiction is quite realistic.

On the lower right is a triggerfish. The grey triggerfish is called *Balistes capriscus*. Triggerfish are found in coral reefs and many of them have wonderful colours. At the very end of his album Coenen presents the first genuine coral fish.

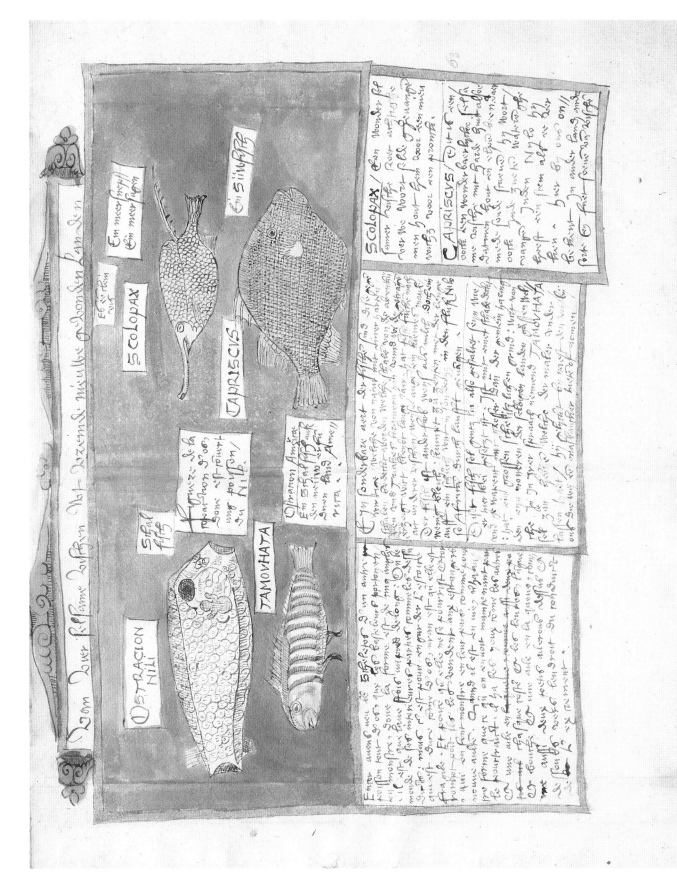

Schuurvis, spiegelvis

The *schuurvis* [abrasive fish] is well known to our fishers in Scheveningen. He is caught in the summer and is also sold here as edible. It is a fish for the poor, not tasty for the rich. He has a rough taste and has a hard, sharp skin like a shark. Some call him a *schuurhaai* [abrasive shark]. The biggest I ever saw was 6 or 7 feet long.

The *spiegelvis* [mirror fish] is well known to our fishers in Scheveningen. He is rarely caught. Our fishers eat him. He has a thin, soft skin with a circular patch on each side like a mirror. Fish like the one illustrated here are sometimes caught in the summer. They are not taken to the fish market, but are kept to be dried as decorations and are sold to city folk as a curiosity. The longest I ever saw was slightly less than 3 feet. 1585.

Coenen's image of the mirror fish is taken directly from Belon.

The angel shark (*Squatina squatina*) is also depicted in Book 1. It can reach 2.5 metres.

The John Dory (*Zeus faber*) probably owes its name to a corruption of *jaune adorée*, that is, the adorable or sacred yellow fish. Characteristic are the fierce gaze, the spot on the side and the tough spines with long threads on the dorsal fins. The John Dory is found in the Mediterranean and on the south-west coast of Great Britain. It is an important commercial fish nowadays.

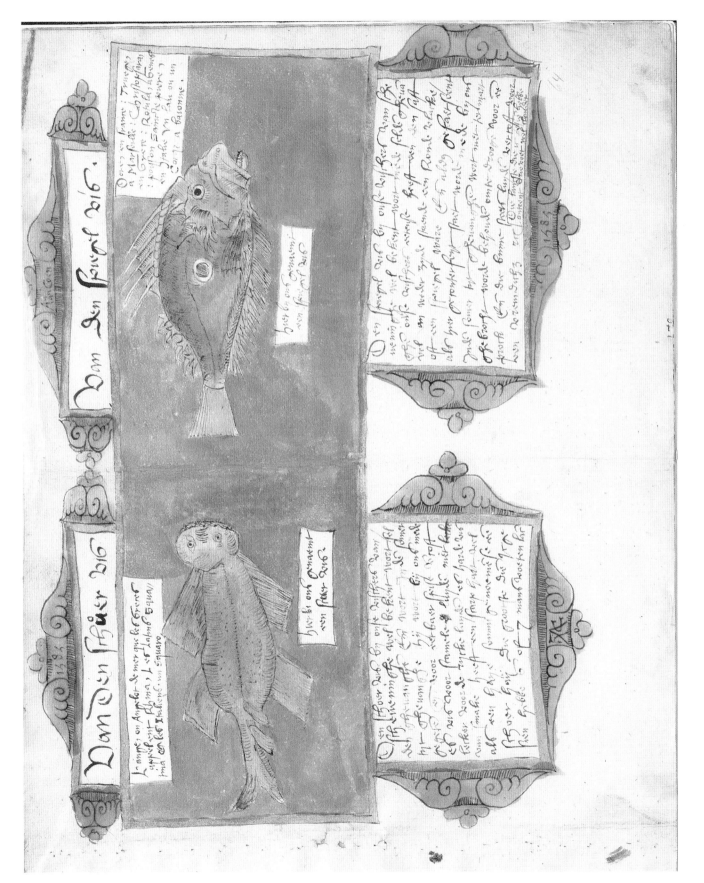

A strange marine creature

This creature is more than ten ells long from head to tail. It was caught on 14 April 1551 near the island of Java and very accurately portrayed. It lives on land and in the water. It is mainly light red in colour, with blue in some places. His tail looks like a horse's tail, is light blue with red spots. He has claws like a lion or panther.

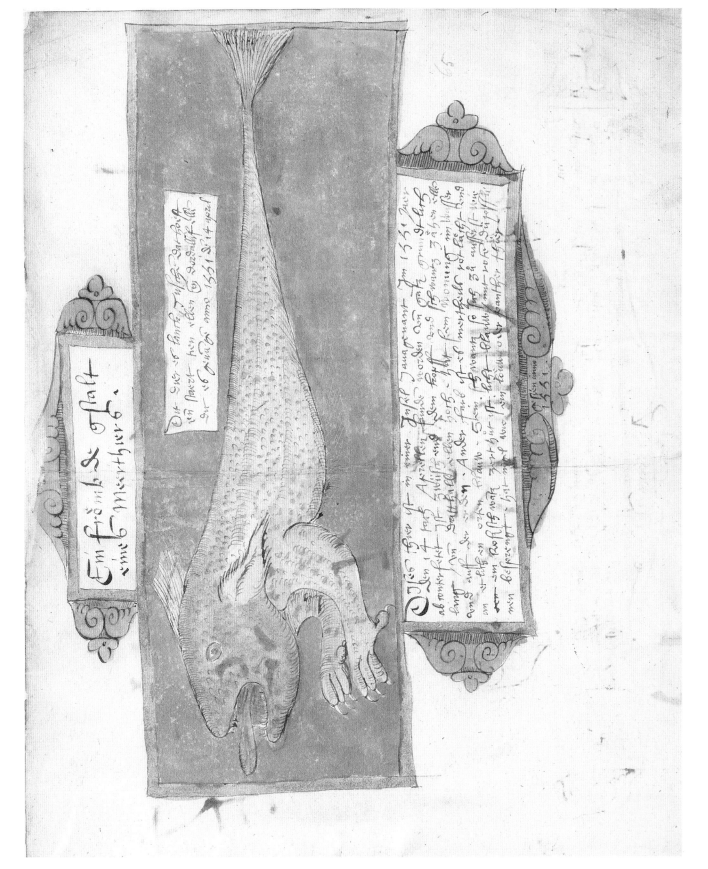

Here are concluded the first two books. Anno 1585.

Hereafter must be compiled with the help of God almighty the third book on the edible and tasty fish that are well known to us here in Holland, as well as other tasty fish in foreign countries that are known to be edible. Adriaen Coenen.